Y0-BEB-177

WALKING NOVA SCOTIA

THE DOER'S AND DREAMER'S COMPLETE GUIDE TO CANADA'S WALKING PROVINCE

BY
BRADFORD W. KETCHUM, JR.
JAY PARIS
CARMI ZONA-PARIS
AND THE EDITORS OF WALKING MAGAZINE

THE WALKING MAGAZINE

BOSTON, MASSACHUSETTS

Published by *The Walking Magazine* in cooperation with
the Nova Scotia Department of Tourism and Culture
and the Nova Scotia Adventure Tourism Association.

Staff:

Chief Editor: BRADFORD W. KETCHUM, JR.
Designer: SUZANNE H. PETERMAN, TOP DOG DESIGN
Writers: JAY PARIS, CARMI ZONA- PARIS
Photographer: WALLY HAYES
Production Director: ROBIN KRAUS

For further information about Nova Scotia, contact:
Nova Scotia Department of Tourism and Culture
136 Commercial Street
Portland, ME 04101
1-800-565-0000

For information on *Walking Magazine* call:
617-266-3322

Cover photograph by Wally Hayes: "Balancing basalt"
on Long Island, near Tiverton (Digby Neck)

Contents

Why Nova Scotia?

I n 1497, after John Cabot landed on the northern coast of Cape Breton Island, he returned to England and proclaimed his discovery of a land edged with many harbours and expansive beaches that rose to majestic highlands.

Cabot was enthralled by the land's fine sand beaches, by eagles soaring overhead and moose emerging from the thick hardwood forests. He wrote of his good fortune in seeing the sun rise above the Atlantic mists, casting its light on harbour seals and seabirds, and of sailing among pilot whales that played in the shimmering waters of the Northumberland Strait. He reported rivers laden with salmon and trout and birds of remarkable variety gathering in woods.

Almost 400 years later, in 1892, one of history's greatest inventors, Alexander Graham Bell, chose to build his summer estate in Nova Scotia, writing, "I have traveled around the globe. I have seen the Canadian American Rockies, the Andes and the Alps, and the Highlands of Scotland; but for simple beauty, Cape Breton Island outrivals them all."

Now, a full century later, Nova Scotia (Latin for *New Scotland*) is still being discovered by visitors who regale in its uncluttered, diverse beauty. They come to walk and hike its coastline, its woodlands and wilderness, and they discover that in five centuries, the "New Scotland" of John Cabot and Alexander Graham Bell still exists. Moose wander abundantly through the province's extensive wilderness, and eagles soar above seals and

Hiker pauses atop Mackenzie Mountain overlooking Pleasant Bay on the Cabot Trail.

whales which still ply its coast in large numbers.

The intervening centuries brought settlements to Nova Scotia which have created a rich heritage, as treasured and preserved as its vast natural resources. Even now, Gaelic is spoken along the renowned Cabot Trail, where descendants of Nova Scotia's early Celtic settlers celebrate their ethnicity with the skirl of bagpipes and flashes of colorful tartans. Between the province's enchanted shores, hikers can explore rugged trails that traverse the wilderness of Cape Breton Highlands National Park or follow coastal trails that rise and fall with the spectacular contours of the mountains.

As many hikers learn, Nova Scotia's landscape is remarkably varied, offering challenges for beginners and experts alike. Below the northern highlands of Cape Breton Island is the 600-mile coastline of Bras d'Or Lake, an exhilarating saltwater inlet that attracts sailors from around the world. The lake is rimmed with woodland trails that climb gentle mountains of mixed coniferous and deciduous trees where migratory birds gather in abundance.

Still farther south of the Cape Breton shore are authentic Acadian fishing villages, centuries old, dotted with brightly colored dories and houses that match. These craggy promontories with cobble and sand beaches support a fascinating assortment of marine life that thrives in the uncrowded environs of their shores.

Nova Scotia's seemingly endless shoreline has become a destination for walkers of every caliber. Many experience a physical and mental renewal in wandering along quiet coves, in the serenity of surf and sea air. The unique blend of spectacular land and open sea, unfettered by development, inspires good health. The air is pristine and quietude is calming. Walking the footpaths is a return to nature where the senses sharpen and the mind eases.

Visitors soon find that each of Nova Scotia's 10 designated areas (see pages 64-65) has been affected by distinct forces of nature but, for walkers, all have the same advantages.

The Lighthouse Route, with its kinship to the jutting Maine coast, and its warm Gulf Stream water, is an inviting feature for any visitor. Quaint fishing villages, historic towns, and miles of fine sand beaches separate an otherwise rocky shore dotted with more than 30 functioning lighthouses. Many who hike this coastline and its historic towns are surprised by its architectural heritage.

Cross-country from the Atlantic shore, the Bay of Fundy's landscape and culture are inextricably tied to the rhythm of the world's highest tides. Hikers who explore the wide beaches will enjoy the extensive bird life, the agates and semiprecious stones, that are waiting to be discovered.

Between these contrasting coastlines is inner Nova Scotia, a wilderness land of lakes and pine forests

WANDER 100 PROVINCIAL PARKS

Nova Scotia has developed an elaborate system of parks as diverse as the landscape it protects.

Created to allow visitors to enjoy the land without harming its natural integrity, more than 100 provincial parks can be found throughout Nova Scotia. Each offers parking and picnic areas, and some are wheelchair accessible.

Hikers will regale in the diversity of well-maintained walking trails that give maximum exposure to wildlife and scenic views. Twenty-one sites allow camping for a small fee and sell firewood.

For information about hiking trails within provincial parks, contact the Nova Scotia Department of Natural Resources, (902) 424-5935.

CHECK IN: WHERE TO STAY

T here are many ways to enjoy overnight stays in Nova Scotia, depending on your tastes and budget. After a long day of walking or hiking, you may enjoy staying at one of 80 Farm and Country vacation homes, each pledged to offer clean, comfortable rooms with bathroom and kitchen facilities.

If you choose to stay in these bucolic places, you will have an opportunity to know a rural family and perhaps participate in its farm activities, livelihood, and recreation. Prices are very rea-

sonable, and it has proven a way to make lifelong friends. For a copy of the Farm and Country Bed and Breakfast Guide, call (902) 883-8496.

Country inns are part of a long tradition of hospitality in Nova Scotia. Many of its inns have maintained the character and graciousness of the past, while still offering modern amenities. From this group of properties, the Nova Scotia Association of Unique Country Inns has named approximately 100 hotels to its most distinguished list. Each displays the emblem of a pineapple, signifying excellence and guaranteeing outstanding accommodations.

For a listing that includes more than 600 government-inspected accommodations, call Check In: (800) 565-0000. Most inns and hotels require a credit card to hold reservations. Be sure to inquire about cancellation and refund policies.

where the Micmacs hunted and fished. Here, with the help of local outfitters, hikers can canoe, fish, and camp in an outback where the subtle pleasures of true wilderness can be readily experienced.

Along the Glooscap Trail, where legend says the Micmacs' man-god still rules, one can explore the watershed of the Cobequid Mountains. Waterfalls cascade into the Minas Basin, where rock-hounding hikers come from all parts of the globe in search of amethysts and fossils.

On the north coast, the Sunrise Trail meets the warm waters of the Northumberland Strait which grace dozens of beaches, attracting swimmers and beachcombers from around the province. Not far away, on the south coast, the Marine Drive takes visitors to Nova Scotia's least frequented area. Living off the beaten track, the families who have fished these Atlantic waters for many generations are congenial and eager to share their stories of the sea.

Because the province is so diverse, it is impossible to discover its many assets in one trip, which is why most walkers and hikers return. It is easy to do. Halifax, the hub of The Maritimes, is a bustling port city that welcomes cruise ships and a full schedule of international flights. By air, Boston, New York, and Baltimore are less than two hours away. Direct flights to Montreal, Detroit, and Toronto are also available daily. Major rental car agencies serve Nova Scotia and accept American and European licenses.

For travelers who wish to come to Nova Scotia by ferry, the *Scotia Prince* leaves Portland, Maine, for Yarmouth each evening, while its sister ship, the *Bluenose*, shuttles between Bar Harbour and Yarmouth. Both ships accommodate vehicles of any size.

Many first-time visitors to Nova Scotia are surprised to discover that the province's southern tip shares the same latitude as southern Maine. Upon arriving, travelers will discover that restaurants offer fresh, wholesome foods and the finest seafood dishes in the world. For accommodations, the province has a wealth of bed and breakfasts, inns, and hotels.

Touring the province is also easy. Pre-trip planners, maps, and guidebooks are easily obtained by calling Check In, the province's computerized travel information and reservation system, or by contacting the Nova Scotia Department of Tourism and Culture (see page 2). After your arrival, visit the many government information centres strategically located throughout the province.

Beauty is a Nova Scotian commodity that its citizens eagerly share. Walkers and hikers who embrace the province's scenic pleasures will find their spirits lifted. By walking its countless byways and trails, they will discover that Nova Scotia is an ideal place to unwind and enjoy unforgettable landscape, engaging wildlife, and hospitable people.

The Day Hiker's Province

N ova Scotia is a province of remarkable choice for walkers and hikers. Contained within its 4,600 miles of coastline is a land about the size of West Virginia with a myriad of opportunities to exercise the body and relax the mind.

Its varied seas and diverse coastlines bring hikers close to harbours, coves, channels, estuaries and lagoons. Just inland from the shore you will find boreal forests typical of the Canadian north, as well as some species of plants and wildlife whose habitats stretch as far south as Louisiana. Nova Scotia is not a large province, but its range of land formations is extraordinary. There are fertile river valleys, wilderness forests, glaciated rock formations, and rugged highlands reminiscent of Scotland. On its western coast, ocean waters rush to the cliffs of the Bay of Fundy twice a day, raising the tides higher than anywhere in the world. As the basin recedes, vast beaches precede even wider mud flats that expose remarkable intertidal life with valuable fossils and semiprecious stones. We encourage you to take the many trails and walks described in this guide to experience Nova Scotia in the healthiest and most intimate way.

You will also discover that Nova Scotia's beauty extends beyond its seascapes and countryside. The province is steeped in history with villages and towns of well preserved homes and welcoming eateries that offer some of the best seafood in the world.

Its cities —Halifax, Dartmouth, Yarmouth, and Sydney, to name a few— offer spectacular museums and large parks to visit and enjoy. Take to Nova Scotia's trails and walkways. Watch eagles float high above spruce forests and whales

frolic in sheltered bays. Share the wooded backcountry with moose and deer and wander to a cove at dusk to enjoy the tranquil panorama of pink clouds hovering over still dories. The array of experiences are endless and uplifting, guaranteeing the traveler on foot a vacation that is as healthy as it is unforgettable.

The following pages offer day hiker planning guides to the great trails in nine regions of the province, Kejimkujik National Park, and the twin cities of Halifax-Dartmouth.

Lighthouse Route

YARMOUTH TO
HALIFAX
VIA SOUTH SHORE

Seacoast Highway 3, the Lighthouse Route, runs along Nova Scotia's south shore passing nearly 30 lighthouses as it meanders past quiet coves where fishermen tie their dories, and sea gulls and seals bob in the surf. Along this coast are historic towns, expansive beaches and some of the province's most stunning vistas.

Inland, you'll find another Nova Scotia of pristine lakes and scenic rivers, deep forests and one of the province's two national parks. For walkers and hikers at every level, this area offers it all — amiable hikes along a remote coast, explorations of villages, hikes through wilderness areas — within easy driving distance of charming bed and breakfasts, unique inns, and delightful restaurants.

YARMOUTH TO CAPE SABLE AREA

For many visitors to Nova Scotia, Yarmouth is their port of entry and where the Lighthouse Route begins. It is here, on the streets of Yarmouth and along the first few miles of Route 3, that first impressions of Nova Scotia are formed. You will immediately discover that the people in Yarmouth, as in all parts of the province, are especially helpful and friendly. You'll also notice that the air is fresh and the food is remarkable. Whether Yarmouth is your first or last stop, it will give you its share of Nova Scotia's best offerings.

If you want to stretch your legs, walk through the historic district, down Main Street and east up Parade and Forest Streets. Enjoy the Victorian homes and shops. Stop at the Yarmouth County Museum, which includes the

Village and lighthouse at Peggy's Cove
are ideal for pause in any walker's day.

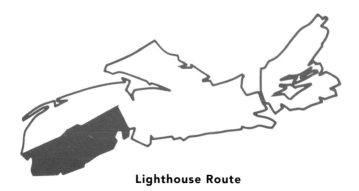

Lighthouse Route

largest collection of ship paintings in Canada and displays an array of seashells that you can collect on beaches that await you on the Lighthouse Route.

There is debate throughout Nova Scotia among cooks and waitresses regarding which town serves the softest and sweetest scallops. Yarmouth, Digby, Lunenburg — all are towns that claim the best. Several restaurants in Yarmouth are well suited to begin your own survey.

For hikers and walkers, there are several excellent day trips from Yarmouth.

Cape Fourchu: Locals boast that this is better than Peggy's Cove and, so far, undiscovered by most tourists. Take Route 304 south nine miles. The rewards are easy parking, back to nature beaches, sand dunes, and exquisite lighthouse view.

Chebogue Meadows Interpretive Trail: If learning about Nova Scotia's wildlife appeals to you, this meticulously preserved area with 12 interpretive stops along its 2.7 mile loop is worth completing. The trail is only 4.2 miles from Yarmouth on Highway 101. Take Highway 340 N. and follow signs.

West Pubnico Coastal Trail: When leaving Yarmouth on the Lighthouse Route, proceed to Pubnico and follow Route 335 S. to the French-speaking fishing village of West Pubnico. The Pubnico villages (Lower West, West, and Middle West) are the oldest Acadian settlements in the world, featuring homes with high, steep roof peaks popularly called the "Acadian Gable." The 4.8- mile trail beginning at a fishing wharf at the end of the village treats walkers to spectacular views of two lighthouses and provides an intimate sense of fishing life and beach ecology. For more directed walking, play golf at the attractive West Pubnico Public Golf Course (18 holes).

SHELBURNE TO LIVERPOOL AREA

One of Nova Scotia's most enchanting qualities is its light. No matter how many times you view the beaches, coves, and fishing villages of the south shore — at late day or early morning, in the shade

Day Hiking Planner

Cape Sable Island Theme Walk

Length: 3.2 km to 19.4 km (2 to 12 mi.), by choice
Time: 1 to 6 hours
Degree of Difficulty: Easy
Special Features: Location of provincial marathon, historic town, and a sunken forest
Amenities: Restaurants and inns
Entrance Point: Along Lighthouse Route, approximately 75 km (47 mi.) from Yarmouth, take causeway (Route 330) to Cape Sable.

Begin walk at head of causeway. In Cape Sable, they say their island is small but their greeting is large. Home of Nova Scotia's marathon where runners complete a figure 8 through the streets of this historic settlement, this is surely a place to explore on foot. Begin by crossing the 3/4-mile long causeway that connects the island to the mainland. You will be touched by the peaceful encounter of running tides, rocky coast, and exquisite fishing hamlets that lay before you.

This special sense of place experienced on the causeway continues as the road bears right toward the village of Centreville. You'll see seals sunning themselves on slick boulders and enjoy a rich array of colorful fishing shacks and homes. Yellow is the color of good luck to Nova Scotia fishermen, which is why it is the predominate color of their dories.

In Centreville, visit the Archelaus Smith Museum, which is a good place to enjoy the marine artifacts of the island and to learn more about its history. There is a sense of history everywhere on Cape Sable, in the preserved homes, the Stone Church in Clark's Harbour, and certainly among its fishing towns. Plan to have lunch in Clark's Harbour.

To explore farther, proceed to the south shore of the island to beachcomb along miles of white sand. The passage of ships in the distance as gulls and seals float nearby is a beguiling sight. At Hawk's Beach, scuba divers can explore a "drowned" forest that disappeared under migrating sand dunes. There is magic on Cape Sable Island. One can see sunrises and sunsets, and experience living history, wonderfully friendly people, and the full bore of the sea.

of bulbous clouds or easing through a mist — the tones change constantly. The light along this shore can be tack sharp, but it can also be diffuse and full of mystery, like the sea that binds it. Along this 50-mile stretch of the Lighthouse Route are opportunities for walkers and hikers not found in any other part of Canada. History has graced it with Shelburne and Lockeport, two notably preserved coastal towns that are best appreciated on foot. Naturalists will be pleased to learn that this area is a major migratory flyway for Canada geese, black ducks, swan, and eider ducks. Coastal hikers, particularly bird-watchers, have very special opportunities to see these waterfowl at close range.

SHELBURNE AND LOCKEPORT

Shelburne and Lockeport are walking towns. Each has published detailed walking guidebooks of their neighborhoods available at their respective tourist information centres.

In 1783, 30 schooners carrying 3,000 outcast British Loyalists arrived from the United States, looking for a place to settle. They chose the deep waters around Shelburne and established its reputation as one of the world's best natural harbours. A boom town was soon created with many streets of impressive Loyalist homes, most of which remain.

Begin your walk on Dock Street. Follow the sidewalks up the hill to the top of the town. You will enjoy the exercise and view. Consider stopping at The Dory Shop, where craftsmen continue to build wooden dories with hand tools in the classic Nova Scotia tradition. Other places of note are the Ross-Thomson House, a museum of Loyalist artifacts and history, and David Nairn House, the official county museum. As your walking tour continues, sample the town's famous cuisine. Every restaurant serves fish chowder made with fresh haddock, scallops, and lobster.

Lockeport, just around the bay, is a town also steeped in history but singularly different from Shelburne. The town sits on an island connected to the mainland by a short causeway. Lockeport's town fathers claim it has more beaches within its city limits than any community in the province. Completely surrounded by water, the town — and entire island — can be walked in a few hours, offering a sprinkling of history with gracious ocean views and exquisite photo opportunities.

Crescent Beach, its lovely white expanse once commemorated on the Canadian $50 bill, lies at the south side of town. Park in this vicinity and head to the historic streetscape where every home has been restored to its original state. If you're a walker with a camera, proceed to the restored railroad trestle at the north end of the village and look back at the town. You will see a harbour of scallop draggers bathed in vibrant colors

❧ Day Hiking Planner ❧

St. Catherine's River Beach

Length: 8 km (5 mi.) round trip
Time: 3 hours
Degree of Difficulty: Easy
Special Features: Seaside adjunct of Kejimkujik National Park; superb bird-watching on migratory flyway; remote beach area
Entrance Point: At Port Joli, go to St. Catherine's River and watch for signs; trail is an old cart track.

It is a pleasant walk through the fir stands to the windswept scrub pines and rock outcrops that begin this trail, but not until the ocean appears do you appreciate the uncommon beauty of St. Catherine's River Beach. The approach is from a 100-foot bluff which overlooks a series of stunning white sand beaches that extend for almost a mile. Just below the bluff is a gathering point for one of the largest colonies of harbour seals on the south shore.

Descend to the rocks for a closer look and then walk along the beaches for a mile and a half. One section may be closed

during the nesting season of the endangered piping plover, a small, shy shorebird that can be seen running along the sand. Still, the magic of this area will not be lessened.

The bogs and marshes behind the beach are major stopover grounds for Canada geese and black ducks. And if you happen to take this walk in mid-summer you may also see sandpipers, whimbrels, and 2,000 featherless eider ducks which molt at this site and bob in the water as they regrow their plumage. Deer also forage throughout the area, and occasionally a black bear or porcupine cross the trail.

— turquoise, yellow, orange, red, and emerald green — quite unlike any other fleet in Nova Scotia.

The trestle bridge will eventually lead you to the fishing hamlet of Lydgate, where you will circle past beaches favored by blue herons. Eventually the road will return you to the causeway and parking areas.

Beyond Lockeport, the Lighthouse Route offers two more walks farther up its coast that are well suited for short visits.

L'Hébert Pocket Wilderness Trail: On Route 103 at the Port Shelburne-Queens County line, in the village of Port l'Hébert (about 12 miles north of Lockeport), is a well-marked trail with parking and picnic area that winds through woods and salt marshes. The 2.2-mile loop gives walkers ample opportunity to see the popular wintering ground of Canada geese, as well as ovenbirds, the common yellow throat and red-eyed vireo.

Pine Grove Trail: In Milton, a town just north of Liverpool on Route 8, there is an area of forests and rivers through which the ancient Micmacs canoed from the ocean. Pine Grove Park is well marked, offering a short but exquisite loop (with wheelchair access) into a stand of white pine with blazing displays of lady's slippers and starflowers. The park also contains extensive duck breeding and resting areas.

BROAD COVE TO PEGGY'S COVE AREA

This section of the Lighthouse Route boasts a surprising mix of picturesque towns, isolated fishing villages, and urbane sophistication. Many residents of this area commute to Halifax, and Michelin Tire has a large factory here. But even with its cosmopolitan connection, it is an unhurried, unspoiled coast with endless beauty and simplicity. Whether traveling along Route 3 or leaving it to walk backroads and discover remote coves, hikers will enjoy the many opportunities to explore this area.

Between Green Bay and the town of Lunenburg, 25 miles up the coast, are three impressive hikes to consider. Although the Lighthouse Route goes north to the river town of Bridgewater, a bustling place with two interesting museums and a reputation for outstanding salmon fishing, you can shorten the route at West La Have by taking a car ferry across the tidal river for a mere 50 cents.

Risser's Beach Provincial Park: On Route 331, you will easily find this distinctive park and its Salt Marsh Trail. The loop, including a visit to Crescent Beach, can be completed in an hour. Highlights are dune habitat, rocky shores, a myriad of bird life, and a boardwalk over a carefully preserved salt marsh.

The Ovens Natural Park: Along Route 103, just eight miles south of Lunenburg, you will find signs directing you to Ovens Natural Park, where an hour's walk has noteworthy benefits. Gold was once mined in this area and occasionally prospectors pan along the

HIKING KEJIMKUJIK'S SEASIDE ADJUNCT

I n 1985, Nova Scotia transferred more than 5,400 acres of land adjacent to the town of Port Mouton to Environment Canada Parks, calling it Kejimkujik National Park's Seaside Adjunct. For hikers who want a true measure of Nova Scotia wilderness, where salt-sprayed forests meet wide sandy beaches, take half a day or so to visit this remote area.

On the Lighthouse Route, travel about 16 miles south of Liverpool on Route 103, then continue south on the St. Catherine's River/Port Joli Road. The road ends in 3.5 miles, at a gravel parking lot, where a path leads through alders to a striking combination of green wilderness and rocky headlands that protrude into emerald coves and broad beaches. Hikers who come to the Seaside Adjunct can explore the coastline in any direction their curiosity takes them.

By following the shore, you may see groups of harbour seals sunning themselves on the rocks. On its extensive beaches, endangered piping plovers breed, and yellowlegs and sandpipers forage for food.

There are no restrooms, water fountains, camping facilities, or other amenities in this wild and scenic area. Take along a water bottle, wear waterproofed hiking boots, and walk into a place that time has not changed, where Nova Scotia is raw and beautiful.

water, attempting to separate valuable nuggets from the large amount of fool's gold that is still scattered along the pebble shore.

The pathway passes many caves or "ovens" which the ocean has carved into the cliffs, and even enters the largest cave where waves create a roar as they rush in below your feet. The park's many tidal pools, glacial outcrops, and vast array of birds make this walk spectacular.

Blue Rocks to Stonehurst: Just four miles south of Lunenburg is Blue Rocks, a fishing village undiscovered by tourists yet unrivaled for quaintness and beauty. Park anywhere along the road and walk among the brightly colored rocks on this stone isthmus that seems perfectly arranged for the artist's brush. After enjoying this hamlet, walk another mile to the equally attractive fishing community of Stonehurst, connected to a small island by a wooden footbridge. From the island, look for a lighthouse which, in wind and fog, seems to be rising out of the sea.

Lunenburg: This is not only one of Nova Scotia's most picturesque towns, it is a fine destination for walkers and hikers to experience incomparable dining and charming accommodations. Lunenburg has the oldest Lutheran and Presbyterian congregations in the country, and its Anglican Church is the second oldest in British Canada. The prominent homes of this town are unrivaled in color and grandness.

Because the town was settled by Swiss, German, and French farmers, its most popular dishes include solomon gundy, Lunenburg pudding, and Lunenburg sausage and sauerkraut complementing choice seafood entrées. Besides its many impressive restaurants, Lunenburg also has a good selection of inns and bed and breakfasts.

Tancook Island Hike: Before leaving Mahone Bay, every serious walker should take an excursion to Tancook Island for at least a day, if not overnight. From the vantage point of this pastoral community, you will see still another side of Nova Scotia life, quite different from the mainland. At Chester on Route 3, there is a passenger ferry that crosses seven miles of Mahone Bay to reach Big Tancook Island. Round trip fare is only $1.00 and takes 50 minutes.

Tancook is a community of 240 people on a 3 1/2- mile-long island, known for its high bluffs, thick woods, and open seascapes. Trails abound.

Peggy's Cove: Before leaving the Lighthouse Route, stop at Peggy's Cove, which is probably the most photographed fishing village in the world. A brisk half- hour walk around its barren but striking perimeter is worth doing, even in the company of other tourists. Don't miss the carving by the late William E. deGarthe, who spent 10 years carving a rock memorial to Canadian fishermen. It is a moving and unique tribute, with a dozen different figures, including the legendary Peggy, gazing out to sea from the large granite boulder.

❧ Day Hiking Planner ❧

Broad Cove To Green Bay

Length: 12.9 km (8 mi.) each way
Time: 3 hours each way
Degree of Difficulty: Moderate
Special Features: Excellent view of offshore islands, very photogenic village and beaches
Amenities: Restaurant, bed and breakfast at start
Entrance Point: Slightly more than halfway up the Lighthouse Route (Route 331) is town of Broad Cove. Park car at South Shore Country Inn. Trail begins at old road that goes behind fishing shacks.

When the Lighthouse Route was constructed, it by-passed a lovely country road that followed the coast between the fishing villages of Broad Cove and Green Bay. The less-used byway became neglected and washed out in places, making passage impossible except on foot.

The road leading away from Broad Cove ambles past brightly colored fishing shacks and then alternately descends to the ocean and ascends up bluffs. Breathtaking panoramas are common, particularly of the LaHave islands and the seals which often play in the surf. In foggy weather, the views, from high and low vantage points, are also alluring. In summer, sandpipers often herd their chicks along the shore in a hurried fashion. In fall, geese and ducks span out overhead, sometimes stopping in nearby salt marshes to feed and rest.

The first sign of the amiable settlement of Green Bay will be fishing dories tied to bright buoys. Stop at the small canteen in town for refreshments and a taste of local news. For a different route back, take the road through the villages of Green Bay and Petite Riviere, which are known for their array of antique and craft shops.

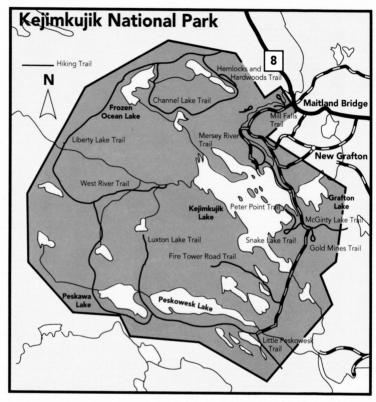

Kejimkujik National Park

Hiking Trail

N

Hemlocks and Hardwoods Trail

8

Frozen Ocean Lake

Channel Lake Trail

Maitland Bridge

Mill Falls Trail

Liberty Lake Trail

Mersey River Trail

New Grafton

West River Trail

Kejimkujik Lake

Peter Point Trail

Grafton Lake

McGinty Lake Trail

Luxton Lake Trail

Snake Lake Trail

Gold Mines Trail

Fire Tower Road Trail

Peskawa Lake

Peskowesk Lake

Little Peskowesk Trail

KEJIMKUJIK NATIONAL PARK TRAILS

For fall hiking in particular, many advocates of walking claim there is no place quite like the inland treks of Kejimkujik National Park in southwestern Nova Scotia.

From the Lighthouse Route at Liverpool, this large, protected wilderness area lies about 74 km (46 mi.) due north on Route 8, attracting canoeists, conservationists, and hikers who enjoy the inland parts of the lower province.

The Kejimkujik area is a glaciated land of rich soil that supported large hardwood forests until settlers and loggers cut them down. It takes several hundred years for stands of oak, eastern hemlocks, ash, and maple to mature. Very few remain and in the last century, red spruce and balsam fir have filled the area's ravines and knolls, shading wild blueberry, bunchberry, and sheep laurel.

Walkers who visit Kejimkujik speak of the mind-clearing treks that this soothing area provides. Along its 120 km (74 mi.) of marked trails, there are lakes and the Mersey River, where beaver and muskrat often frolic. In a canoe, paddling quietly through the unruffled water, it is hard to believe that the harsher, open coast of the Atlantic is a mere hour away.

The rangers advise that fall is the best time of year to visit Kejimkujik. Fall is a time of cool nights and warm days, dry trails, and blazing color. Visitors to Kejimkujik will find that by autumn, the bugs are gone. The park offers over a dozen trails ranging from 3 to 28 km (2 to 17 mi.) in length, on gentle terrain, that are all a pleasure to walk. Here are two:

Mersey River Trail *(photo below)*: Approximately 14.5 km (9 mi.) of easy terrain and considerable tranquility. Enter trail from the Heber Meadow section of the park. Expect to see beavers, muskrat, deer, and the rare blanding turtle, which thrives only in this small part of Atlantic Canada.

Big Dam Frozen Ocean Trail: 21 km (13 mi.), beginning at well-marked point near park opening. Unforgettable inland hike that includes a walk through a hemlock forest.

Evangeline Trail

The Evangeline Trail, named for the heroine of Longfellow's epic poem about the Acadians, courses its way along the Bay of Fundy. With its unique blend of provincial heritage and tidal shores, hikers and walkers are not only treated to a striking landscape of high bluffs overlooking bogs and tidal pools, but also rare wildflowers and one of the most visible whale populations in the world.

DIGBY TO BRIER ISLAND AREA

The drive along the Bay of Fundy to Digby has an imperturbable quality that gives added meaning to maritime. Visits to this land should not be rushed. Mari-"time" is more than an hour ahead of the rest of Canada and the United States. It is also a state of mind— self-composed, steady, and unruffled — like the communities that are nestled along the bay.

The town of Digby, a community of 2,500 hospitable people, serves as the metropolitan hub of the Evangeline Trail. It has a championship golf course, a well-equipped hospital, excellent restaurants and inns, and one of the largest scallop fleets in the world. As much as south shore chefs boast about their scallops, Digby residents claim that no one has bigger, softer, and more delectable varieties. Before judging, try a scallop sauteed in butter from a Digby kitchen. Visit Fisherman's Wharf, explore the harbour, and converse with men who work at sea.

A short drive out to Prim Point offers more remote walks with sweeping views of the bay and its

On a bird watch, this couple enjoys the countryside near Grand Pré, off Route 1.

Evangeline Trail

tall lighthouse. Or, if you seek a truly unique Nova Scotia getaway off the beaten track, travel down Digby Neck, a premier destination for hikers and walkers. Take Highway 217 along the Bay of Fundy shoreline to Sandy Cove, a village nestled between two sand beaches often visited by rock hounds.

Sandy Cove Walks: When the 30-foot tides of this area drop, walkers often hunt for agates, jasper, and even amethysts which reveal their telltale quartz on the cliff sides. The topography of the area is varied. On one side of the isthmus there are sloping fields; on another is Mt. Shubel, named for the biblical hill in Israel, where one can see the distant spouting of finback whales frolicking beneath the distant outline of New Brunswick.

After visiting Sandy Cove, walkers will appreciate crossing two short channels by ferry. The cost is only $1.00 round trip to visit ecologically unique Brier Island.

Brier Island: Considering that this land mass is only three miles in circumference, it teems with wildlife, fauna, and hiking opportunities. Birds from three flyways—Canada, Europe, and the Arctic—cross its path in spring and fall.

The largest flights of the 130 species typically sited are puffins, grebes, kittiwakes, and razorbills. The trails of the interior island are vibrantly decorated by wildflowers, highlighted by 15 varieties of wild orchids and bright scatterings of mountain avens, a yellow flower found only here and in the White Mountains of New Hampshire.

Westport, the island's village, is home port for a large fishing fleet. Because the water flowing into the Bay of Fundy is highly saline, it brings large amounts of zooplankton which attract herring and mackerel. They, in turn, attract whales and dolphins in striking numbers. Whale watching boat tours are offered daily, with sightings guaranteed.

After enjoying this striking area, return to the Evangeline Trail and proceed past Digby to Annapolis Royal, Canada's oldest town.

Annapolis Royal: Founded in 1605, this unblemished village is a testament to preservation and good planning. Its streets and homes maintain their historical integrity while serving thousands of tourists each year. Walkers can take a self-guided 45-minute tour called "Footprints and Footnotes," available at most businesses and at the

Day Hiking Planner

Delaps Cove Trails

Length: 7.2 km total (2 and 2.5 mi.)
Time: 2 hours round trip
Degree of Difficulty: One loop easy; one loop difficult on very rocky, uneven terrain
Special Features: Remote wilderness area
Amenities: Restroom at entrance
Entrance Point: North from Annapolis Royal, off Route 1, to Parkers Cove, then west to Delaps Cove. Follow signs to Delaps Cove Wilderness Trail. Parking lot at entrance.

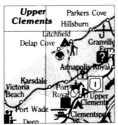

According to the 1871 census, the Delaps Cove area was once a thriving settlement of freed slaves who were given land grants along this remote section of the Bay of Fundy. Now their farms are wilderness, divided by a rock-strewn logging road from which two inviting trails begin.

The first, called Bowhaker, is a two-mile oval that starts on a low escarpment of rocks overlooking the Bay of Fundy. Soon it merges into a forest, richly embedded with ferns, especially the Christmas tree fern which stands almost four feet high and resembles its namesake to a remarkable degree. Half way through the walk, the trail issues onto the bay shoreline amidst seaside golden rods and beach tea while bands of sea gulls bob in the light surf. After half a mile, the path winds back into the dense spruce and pine woods.

Heartier walkers should consider a second 2 1/2-mile loop called Charlie's Trail, which begins a mile or two farther down the craggy logging road. It is more rigorous and less visited, with a harsh, granite terrain that requires sturdy footwear.

Nova Scotia's quality of remoteness is well reflected in the pristine setting of Delaps Cove. It is a place that clears the mind and enables trekkers to be attentive to nothing more than the interplay of forest light and the faint honks of black ducks echoing through the forests. Passage through these wooded shores is a taste of Nova Scotia that shouldn't be missed.

town's tourist information centre. There is a placid rhythm to the Evangeline Trail. Small, historic towns give way to a remote, moody coastline filled with a rich array of marine life. Not far from Annapolis Royal, in Delaps Cove, walkers can experience that haunting spirit of Evangeline on two wilderness trails.

COLDBROOK TO WOLFVILLE AREA

Between Coldbrook, Wolfville, and the spectacular lookoffs at Cape Blomidon, one finds Nova Scotia's prize-winning dairy farms and sprawling apple orchards. And in this valley of Micmac legends and new world settlements, every town has a story to tell. In Coldbrook and Kentville, it is of apples and cold, sweet cider, made on hillside farms. Between these two towns, turn off Route 1 (the Evangeline Trail) and explore the back roads. Park your car and walk a few miles, enjoying the crossing patterns of apple trees climbing to the horizon.

From Coldbrook and Kentville, the land changes to a different kind of farming, with open pastures and steeper hills. It is among these foothills that one comes to Wolfville.

Wolfville Town Hike: Wolfville is a rustic university town of charming Victorian homes, located on the Minas Basin. Twice each day, 50-foot tides literally empty its harbour, leaving boats along its waterfront lying starkly in mud or,

12 hours later, bobbing in deep water, vividly picturesque. Because Wolfville adjoins the farmlands of the Annapolis Valley, its restaurants offer fresh fruits, vegetables, and meats, year-round. Choices for overnight stays in Wolfville are plentiful and rewarding.

Dike Walk between Wolfville and Grand Pre': One of the most rewarding hikes from Wolfville starts at the town's visitor information centre on Route 1, where the beginning of a vast dike system was built two centuries ago to curb the tides of Minas Basin. Made of clay, this slight elevation of dirt was constructed by enterprising Acadian farmers. Today, hikers can walk the tops of the dikes from Wolfville to the town of Grand Pre', about two miles away, observing cows foraging on one side of the dikes while lobster boats motor nearby along the shore. Rarely will you have a more intimate sense of the tides rising and falling or view marine life at such close range.

For more information about walking the dike system, contact the Wolfville Visitor's Centre, (902) 542-7000.

From Wolfville and Grand Pre', the Annapolis Valley forms a remarkable cape which heads into the Minas Basin, splitting it from the Bay of Fundy. Route 358 to this exquisite land formation goes by Scots Bay, a rock hound's paradise on a crescent stone beach, and finally dead-ends where one of Canada's most famous trails, Cape Split, begins.

✺ Day Hiking Planner ✺

Cape Split Trail

Length: 12.9 km (8 mi.) round trip
Time: 2 1/2 hours out and 2 hours return
Degree of Difficulty: Moderate with slight incline out; bumpy, rooted trails
Special Features: Erosion at edge of bluffs makes footing dangerous off main trail. Single access to beach but very dangerous if caught by incoming tides away from access point
Amenities: None
Entrance Point: At end of Route 358, beyond Scots Bay

Far up the Bay of Fundy, between the Minas Channel and Minas Basin, is a trek that many consider to be one of the most spectacular walks in North America. It is not difficult terrain, but the trek takes six or seven hours if you travel at a leisurely pace and stop at intervals to enjoy the extraordinary vistas.

To reach the Cape Split trail, follow Route 358 north, which intersects the Evangeline Trail between Kentville and Wolfville. Follow past Scots Bay to dead end. The main trail, which begins at a parking lot, veers off to the right. The path winds through deciduous and coniferous forests, rising gently as it traverses the cape and offers inspirational glimpses of two very different seas. To the west is the Bay of Fundy, raw and exposed with swift tides driving into its cliffs. To the east is the Minas Basin, a green sea of unruffled waters and long red mud flats where even the sunlight is always tranquil.

Deer sometimes cross the path and eagles call out as they soar above the water in search of fish. During the last half mile of the trail, trees fall away and the high moors of the ever narrowing cape open to a view that makes the long walk so worth taking. From atop the bluffs, the unspoiled sky, the two broad mains, one serene and one churning, and the distant promontories of the Glooscap Trail come together. Here one understands why the Micmacs claim that the original Glooscap, their mythical god, lived on this spot, watching over his "children of light."

After savoring the uplifting power of this panorama, you'll understand why visitors to this part of Nova Scotia always want to return.

Glooscap Trail

The Glooscap Trail faces the mighty tides of the Bay of Fundy, where fossils and semiprecious agates emerge from the great mud flats and eagles circle the land. This is a place of legends and sacred Indian grounds where beauty continually greets the eye like a kaleidoscope.

BURNTCOAT HEAD TO WENTWORTH

The lower Glooscap Trail traces the Minas Basin where the low tides reveal broad, muddy shores. Route 215, the Glooscap Trail highway between Brooklyn and Truro, intersects the woodlands and farms of this sparsely populated area, passing the villages of Walton, Tennycape, Minasville, and Noel. About half a mile beyond Minasville, a secondary road turns left (north) and loops around a jut of land known as Burntcoat Head.

Burntcoat Head: This serene seven-mile stretch of fields and pine groves sits precisely at the spot where the Bay of Fundy tides reach their greatest extremes (55 feet). To enjoy this natural phenomenon, continue around Burncoat Head for five miles to a small parking lot with signs that indicate the area is protected for migratory birds. From the parking lot, walkers will enjoy this muddy beach which extends out for a mile at low tide. If you enjoy eating clams, consider rolling up your pants and digging your own. Nova Scotia does not require permits or licenses, and the beds throughout this area are highly productive.

Beachcombing for driftwood and fossils is also popular here, but a note of caution: the tides rise an inch per minute or five feet an

There's nothing quite like walking along a Fundy beach at low tide (here at Baxter Harbour).

Glooscap Trail

hour. Don't get caught too far from shore in these waters which rarely top 10° C (50 ° F).

Truro: Highway 215 continues to Route 2, which quickly enters the bustling town of Truro, the geographical centre of Nova Scotia. Although Truro is known for many firsts, including the first felt hats made in Canada (1865) and the production of the world's first pair of knitted ribbed underwear (1877), walkers should not miss Victoria Park, one of the province's finest urban parks. Take Brunswick Avenue east from Route 2 and follow signs to the park's entrance. From the parking lot, follow a central trail through a gorge with an aged hardwood forest to a series of tranquil waterfalls. The round trip can be accomplished in an hour and makes for a great warm-up to the many seafood dishes which Truro restaurants offer.

Depending on your timing, you may also want to stop along the banks of the Salmon River, where visitors often gather to watch the half-foot wave that builds when the steep tides cause the river to run backward. In truth, it is a quiet event, even if unique to rivers that flow into the Bay of Fundy, which can be monitored by calling DIAL-A-TIDE at (902) 426-5494.

As Route 2 departs from Truro, the banks of the Minas Basin become steeper, rising into foothills that farmers have subdivided into pastures. For firsthand experience of walking in these higher elevations, follow Route 104 north, where it intersects Route 2 at the village of Glenholme. Within 15 miles, you will come to Ski Wentworth, one of Nova Scotia's alpine ski areas with 18 miles of trails fanning out across the eastern edge of the Cobequid Mountains. From spring through fall, these trails make excellent day hikes through the woods and occasional farmlands of central Nova Scotia.

Wentworth Youth Hostel Trail: This is one of the best two-hour (3.5 miles) loops on the Glooscap Trail, traversing hilly terrain that is sometimes quite steep but offers terrific views of adjacent hills and valleys. From Highway 104, turn west at the south end of Wentworth Provincial Picnic Park.

❧ Day Hiking Planner ❧

Five Islands Provincial Park

Length: 10.4 km (6.5 mi.) total; 3 trails
Time: From 1 hour to 2 1/2 hours (5 hours total)
Degree of Difficulty: Easy, moderate, and strenuous
Special Features: 13 spectacular views of Minas Basin
Amenities: Restrooms and water
Entrance Point: On Route 2, just east of community of Five Islands

On the south side of Route 2 near Five Islands, the province has established a 1,117-acre park on a mystical headland at the foot of Economy Mountain. The park boasts three walking trails that will appeal to hikers of every level. The shortest, Gorge Trail, is a mere mile long, but it is very steep as it passes through deep green gorges and massive hardwoods. The second walk, on Estuary Trail, is 2.5 miles long and moves along a river valley amidst thick stands of birch and fir. The third loop, Red Head Trail, is three miles long and winds through hills and dales of spruce forests to 13 separate and spectacular views of the Minas Basin. From many vantage points along this trail it is easy to understand why the Micmacs believed these promontories to be sacred.

This is the heart of Glooscap country, towering above the sea, half in a higher world of Indian spirit. Glooscap was the man-god of magic who, legend claims, was mocked by an animal spirit named Beaver. The angry god scooped up land from the gorges and heaved it at Beaver, creating five islands in the bay. Moose Island, the largest, has other legends of pirate treasures attached to it. No matter how many hours or days you spend along the Minas Basin on the Glooscap Trail, when viewed from the park trails, it is different. Natives claim it is a matter of height, of closeness to the water, and some say, of magic. But whatever the combination, it is unquestionably intriguing and beautiful to all of its visitors.

10 GREAT SPOTS FOR CANOEING AND KAYAKING

1. **Shubenacadie River:** Canoe rentals at Enfield. Upper sections suitable for easy paddling; experience needed as river widens at mouth of Cobequid Bay.
2. **Mersey River:** Two hours from Halifax; at Kejimkujik National Park. Canoe rentals at Jake's Landing. Easy paddling upriver for about 2 miles. Ideal for novices.
3. **Bras d'Or Lake:** Sheltered areas include River Denys Basin; West Bay; Washabuck River; St Andrew's Channel. Canoe and kayak rentals at Dundee.
4. **Stewiacke River:** Rentals at Lansdowne Lodge, Upper Stewiacke. Stewiacke is slow-moving river, empties into Shubenacadie.
5. **Musquodoboit River:** A Class II river best run in spring or early summer. Canoe rentals at Meagher's Grant. Several put in and take out areas; an hour's drive from Halifax-Dartmouth.
6. **Spry Bay:** Ocean canoeing and kayaking. Instruction and guided tours available from Coastal Adventures. Safe ocean paddling around islands, peninsulas, and headlands. Lots of seabirds and marine mammals.
7. **Clyde River:** Easy-going stream flows through woodlands and fields. Canoe rentals and overnight trips available from Maritime Canoe Outfitters in Shelburne.
8. **LaHave River:** Best run in spring and early summer. White-water sections. Requires experience. Excellent salmon fishing.
9. **Annaplois River:** Class I stream meanders through lush farmland of Annapolis Valley. Historic towns and villages along the way. Canoe rentals at Annapolis River Campgrounds, Bridgetown.
10. **Salmon River:** Slow meandering stream wends its way through unpopulated woods. Access from Two Rivers Wildlife Park near Marion Bridge, south of Sydney.

For further information contact: Canoe Nova Scotia 5516 Spring Garden Rd. Box 3010, South Halifax, NS B3J 3G6

At Station Road, turn left. The hostel and entrance to the trails are half a mile away.

The upper Bay of Fundy along this section of the Glooscap Trail is one of Nova Scotia's most dramatic coastlines. The Cobequid Mountains rise over the Minas Basin, forming a vast watershed laced with streams that cascade into the sea. The Micmacs have always held these mountains to be magical and claim that their spirit god, Glooscap, emerged to rule their world.

Visitors often perceive the mystical quality of beauty that pervades the woods and shoreline. Rock collectors diligently walk its tidal flats in search of agate, jasper, zeolite, and amethyst which the Micmacs say are a gift from Glooscap, who threw them onto the shore. Fossil collectors also congregate in the area to search for relics of prehistoric creatures. Significant finds are not unusual. In 1985, the largest cache of fossilized bones found in North America was discovered near Parrsboro.

Economy Falls Trail: Economy Falls is a stunning waterfall of almost 90 feet, where the Economy River tumbles out of Economy Mountain. The 2.5-mile trail leads into a gorge of rustic steps, delicately marked by Canada lilies and mayflowers. The waterfall is audible for much of the walk and when it finally appears, crystalline and

clear, it is breathtaking. There are many rock outcrops to sit on and contemplate the falling water spilling into the quiet trout pools below.

The trip out of the gorge offers a different perspective on plant life, particularly the area's aged sugar maples. No less impressive is the ride down the mountain road to Route 2, past open fields of blueberries toward the long reach of Minas Basin. To reach Economy Falls, turn off Route 2 near Upper Economy on River Philip Road (north). Follow it for four miles to signs for Economy Falls. A highly visible trail enters the steep gorge.

Wards Fall Trail: From Parrsboro, take Highway 209 west toward Diligent River for 4.2 miles. After crossing two bridges, turn right onto a small dirt lane where a sign for Wards Fall Trail is posted. The trail is an exceptionally beautiful walk up a long river gorge of 2.4 miles on a good but steep trail. The trail crosses the Diligent River several times but is mostly in a dense woods with spectacular ferns. Near the end of the trail, while traversing the valley floor, a 10-foot waterfall emerges which signals the uphill leg of the walk.

Parrsboro is the cultural hub of this section of the Glooscap, offering many good eateries and inns. If you happen to be in town on a Sunday evening in July, take a sandwich and cold drink to the town green to listen to the Parrsboro Town Band concerts. They start at 7 p.m. sharp, as they have since 1938.

Sunrise Trail

Throughout the Sunrise Trail region, the majority of walking and hiking opportunities occur at the beaches and towns on the Northumberland Strait. Traditionally, Nova Scotians refer to beaches as breaks in their rocky coast, which are often stone and pebble; but, along the Sunrise Trail, many are filled with a fine white sand.

Because of its shallow basin, the waters of the Northumberland Strait reach 20° C (70° F) each summer, making it a favored spot for vacationers. Summer cottages are popular from Tidnish Head, at the New Brunswick border, to New Glasgow, halfway up the Sunrise Trail. Inland, the mineral rich soil is prime agricultural land for dairy and cattle farms, some of which roll down to the shore.

It is often said that every visitor to Nova Scotia should become lost at least once. The relatively flat topography south of the Sunrise Trail is laced with secondary roads that lead past lakes and rivers, interconnecting small towns with Celtic names. It is worth wandering to discover the back-road farm stands with their fresh array of newly picked fruits and vegetables, and to enjoy unhurried browsing in bucolic country stores.

In the midst of this farmland, at the bottom of River Philip, where Routes 321 and 301 join, is the town of Oxford. Known as the wild blueberry capital of Nova Scotia, this village of 1,470 people holds a blueberry festival in late August that features pies, ice cream, tarts, muffins, and cakes that any berry connoisseur should not miss. From Oxford, return to the shore along Route 321,

Beaches are the byword on the Sunrise Trail.
This is Melmerby, northeast of New Glasgow.

Sunrise Trail

which comes to the harbour towns of Pugwash and Wallace Bay.

Wallace Bay National Wildlife Area: The beach at the end of this 3.2-mile loop is a good place to swim or wade after enjoying the 1.2-mile wildlife trail that begins west of the village of Wallace on Route 6, along the Sunrise Trail. Signs for the park are well marked. The trail begins in a serene wooded section before joining a dike where waterfowl and songbirds gather in large numbers.

WALLACE TO PICTOU

The Sunrise trip east along Route 6 passes Tatamagouche Bay and Waterside Beach and into Pictou (pop. 4,413), one of the area's largest coastal towns. The lobster is a specialty here, celebrated with a festival in early July. Pictou is also Nova Scotia's original Gaelic community where, in 1773, 33 Scottish families and 25 unmarried men began the wave of Scottish immigration to the area they dubbed "New Scotland." The town's many streets are lined with 18th century homes. In walking Pictou, don't miss its informative museums, including the architecturally unique Northumberland Fisheries Museum.

Beach walks across the Sunrise Trail are enhanced by the variety of scenes that occur in rapid succession. One minute you will be on a ridge overlooking a farm, the next minute, passing by a salt marsh protected by scenic dikes. When traveling east on Route 245, after leaving New Glasgow, the low lying lands begin to elevate. At Cape George, the high banks overlooking the sea reach an impressive 623 feet, this section of the Sunrise Trail popularly known as "The Mini Cabot Trail." While enjoying this diverse region, consider exploring the following:

Merigomish Island Beach: Look for a sign for Merigomish Island, 9.3 miles east of New Glasgow on the Sunrise Trail (Route 245). The small road north crosses onto a slim isthmus of 3.3 miles, which offers walkers numerous entrance points onto a long sand beach which can be explored for hours. **Pomquet Beach:** About 9.3 miles east of Antigonish on Highway 104, between exit 35 and 36, watch for signs to Pomquet and Pomquet Beach. On St. George's Bay, this 1.9-mile sandy beach has one of Canada's few dunes that is gaining size. Parking and restroom facilities are excellent. Fitness walkers will enjoy the nearly 4-mile total hike up and back.

❧ Day Hiking Planner ❧

Pictou Island

Length: 16.5 km (10.2 mi.)
Time: 8 hours
Degree of Difficulty: Moderate
Special Features: 5-mile-long island with diverse migratory birds, excellent beaches, and picturesque views
Amenities: None
Entrance Point: The island is reachable only by passenger ferry from the wharf at Caribou (where ferry to Prince Edward Island also departs) on Route 106 north of Pictou. Fee is $1 each way for 20-minute ride.

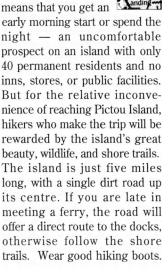

The ferry from Caribou to Pictou Island runs only on Tuesday, Thursday, and Friday, making two trips each day. The first is at 7:00 a.m. and the second is at 5:00 p.m., which means that you get an early morning start or spend the night — an uncomfortable prospect on an island with only 40 permanent residents and no inns, stores, or public facilities. But for the relative inconvenience of reaching Pictou Island, hikers who make the trip will be rewarded by the island's great beauty, wildlife, and shore trails. The island is just five miles long, with a single dirt road up its centre. If you are late in meeting a ferry, the road will offer a direct route to the docks, otherwise follow the shore trails. Wear good hiking boots.

In perambulating the 10.2-mile circumference of the island, the shore is sometimes rocky and rough and, at other times, flat and smooth. Add a picnic lunch, plenty of water, a bathing suit, and binoculars to your daypack staples. The island's northern shore has two fine, white sand beaches, as inviting as any sunbathing areas in Nova Scotia. On the eastern shore, seals are commonly seen resting on rocks as migratory birds produce a considerable chorus of songs.

Pictou Island is a place for walkers and hikers who want to leave the beaten path. After a day of hiking its remote shoreline, you will have a poet's sense of the Northumberland Strait and the wildlife that is part of it.

FOR BIRDING, TRY AMHERST POINT

Located near the New Brunswick border at the head of the Bay of Fundy, the Amherst Point Migratory Bird Sanctuary is a mosaic of ponds, marshes, forests, and old farm fields. Known among geologists for its sinkholes, or conical depressions, the series of mineral-rich ponds has become one of Canada's finest bird watching areas.

The sanctuary is located on a migratory flyway and provides habitat for an impressive variety of hawks, owls, songbirds, and shorebirds. Each spring, Nova Scotia's first migratory arrivals land at Amherst Point, including the Virginia rail, black tern, and American coot.

If wildlife photography interests you, the Amherst Point Migratory Bird Sanctuary offers many unusual opportunities. You can photograph birds on still, reflective waters or against the setting sun. The area, which covers more than 1,200 acres, has miles of trails that follow the shoreline through woods and abandoned pastures.

5 GREAT AREAS FOR ANGLERS

- **Margaree River:** West side of Cape Breton Island; best fishing in July and Sept. to mid-Oct.; world-class salmon fishing

- **Lake Ainslie:** Just west of Bras d'Or Lake, on Cape Breton Island; speckled trout fishing with many streams on southeast section

- **St. Mary's River:** On Route 7 (Marine Drive), near Sherbrooke; best fishing mid-June to end of Aug.; one of North America's renowned salmon rivers

- **Mersey River:** Off Lighthouse Route, Route 8 at Liverpool, toward Lake Rossignol; famous for brown trout; numerous salmon pools

- **Stewiacke River:** On Route 289, off Route 2 at Brookfield (between Halifax and Truro); brown trout and salmon (salmon season mid-Sept. to mid-Oct.)

5 GREAT ROCKHOUNDING AREAS

- **Joggins:** 20 miles south from Amherst, on Route 242 (Glooscap Trail); tidal flats, cliffs, fossils, guided tours

- **Parrsboro:** Large town on Route 2 (Glooscap Trail); area of recent important fossil discoveries; rockhound round-up in early August

- **Arisaig Provincial Park:** On Route 245 (Sunrise Trail), 20 miles north of New Glasgow; provincial park with beach access to fossil area

- **The Ovens Natural Park:** On Route 332 (Lighthouse Route), former gold mining area with sea caves; gold and fool's gold still found

- **Scots Bay:** Route 358, off Evangeline Trail; 15 miles north of Wolfville, on Minas Basin; tidal flats with agates and amethysts

URBAN
HIKER'S
GUIDE TO

Halifax-Dartmouth

H alifax is a multi-cultured city, bound by a history that spans 250 years. Today, its diverse citizens share their contagious enthusiasm for its museums, historical buildings, scenic parks, and fashionable malls. With a multiplicity of guided and do-it-yourself walking tours available each day, visitors are heartily welcomed.

Halifax was constructed on a hill that rises from a well-preserved and historic harbour. At its apex is one of North America's finest public gardens and a grandly preserved fortress. Along the way you will pass three bustling universities, outstanding examples of high Victorian architecture, and cosmopolitan stores and restaurants. Halifax has always brimmed with activity. In 1749, Colonel Edward Cornwallis of the British military founded Halifax at the insistence of New Englanders who feared the ominous French presence on Cape Breton Island.

A seaport and garrison town from its inception, Halifax's natural harbour has offered a welcome respite to ships of all nations.

To appreciate its preservation, one must also consider how close Halifax came to total destruction in the fall of 1917, when a Belgium relief ship collided with a French munitions ship in its harbour. The resulting fire ignited five million pounds of explosives which leveled 1,600 buildings, killed 2,000 people, and injured 6,000 more. Through countless acts of bravery, the citizens of Halifax extinguished the fires and helped the injured. As other regions of the world learned of their plight, aid arrived from all

Bandstand at Halifax Public Gardens is centerpiece for oldest Victorian gardens in North America.

Halifax-Dartmouth

corners of the globe. As a way of thanking the particularly generous citizens of New England, Nova Scotia began a tradition of giving the city of Boston its official Christmas tree which is ceremoniously lit each December.

To best appreciate the history and resources of Halifax, be sure that any guided tour you take includes the Province House, Nova Scotia Museum, Public Gardens, Saint Paul's Church, and Halifax City Hall.

If you prefer a self-guided tour, begin at a section of the harbour on Upper Water Street, called Historic Properties. Within this group of restored warehouses dating back to the early 1800's is the Maritime Museum of the Atlantic and a convenient office of the Nova Scotia Department of Tourism and Culture. Both places are well suited to orienting you to the city's past and present, with maps and pamphlets available at no cost. And don't forget to visit the mayor for tea every weekday afternoon between 3:30 and 4:30. No appointments are necessary, and everyone is welcome.

For more variety and exercise, ascend the Citadel footsteps where even a fit walker will get a challenging workout climbing to this 19th century British fortress that overlooks the city. Tour the impeccably maintained public gardens, featuring a large display of formal Victorian plantings, or, if you wish to sample more of Halifax's natural environment, take an excursion to Point Pleasant Park. This 186-acre refuge away from the bustle of the city has miles of walking trails with great seaside panoramas, small forests, and even sandy swimming beaches.

DARTMOUTH: MORE THAN A TWIN CITY

When visiting Halifax, don't overlook its sister city just a short ferry ride away. Dartmouth (pop. 65,000), Nova Scotia's second largest metropolis, has a notable heritage all its own. More residential than Halifax, the city climbs a hill above Halifax Harbour where you can wander past many fine examples of Victorian architecture.

For walkers, Dartmouth offers several highlights that should not be missed. At its waterfront, there are boardwalks that lead east and west from the Dartmouth Ferry Terminal, providing superb views of McNabs Island, Georges Island, and Halifax's growing skyline. First connecting the two cities in 1752, the terminal is the site of the oldest saltwater ferry system in North America. Today, Dartmouth residents ferry back and forth to Halifax for a mere 75 cents each way. And on a moonlit evening, with a soft summer breeze lifting off the waters, nothing is more pleasant.

On the Dartmouth side, one can take free historic walking tours from Ferry Terminal Park, conducted daily in July and August. Check with the ferry office at the waterfront for specific times.

Within the city, hikers also will find an array of well-developed trails. From June 1 to Labour Day, visit the Fairbanks Interpretive Centre, which is well marked along Waverly Road. The centre has reconstructed two of the locks for the infamous Shubenacadie Canal, which was built in 1852 to link the Bay of Fundy with the Atlantic waters of the southern shore. You will also enjoy a stroll along the restored canal walk in Shubie Park, which can be covered in 30 minutes.

If getting away from it all without leaving the city is appealing, consider a day trip to Laurie Park on Route 2. This provincial park has excellent fishing in Grand Lake and is an enjoyable spot for picnics and shoreline strolls. Still another walk along water can be found along the eastern tip of Dartmouth, where Rainbow Haven Beach offers a striking expanse of sand, dune walks, and Nova Scotia's best beach volleyball.

With their illustrious pasts and positive futures, Halifax and Dartmouth offer something for everyone, and always with legendary Nova Scotian hospitality. When it comes to accommodations, you will find many outstanding choices. To determine the best setting for your needs, call Check In, the province's free computerized reservation and travel information service available seven days a week, (800) 565-0000.

Halifax's night lights are captured from Dartmouth waterfront.

Marine Drive

The Marine Drive follows the many contours of Nova Scotia's eastern shore as it passes fishing villages, sandy beaches, and remote sections of forests. This area of the province has changed the least in the last few decades—it is less known and, therefore, has been less affected by tourists.

Much of the charm of the Marine Drive is its remoteness and simplicity. The unchanged traditions along this coast were formed many generations ago by fishing families whose progeny continue to make their living from the sea. In driving this alternate route to Cape Breton, enjoy the subtleties of landscape and culture of these friendly people. Enjoy the beaches and the opportunities to fish and canoe along the many lakes and rivers. Although the number of hikes along the Marine Drive are fewer than other areas, the walks that follow are well worth taking.

Musquodoboit Harbour: As the largest settlement (pop. 930) along the western section of the Marine Drive, this village lies 15.5 miles east of Dartmouth and offers walkers a notable array of activities. The town is divided by a popular salmon and trout stream which anglers can enjoy with guides and equipment rented locally.

From late fall through spring, one of the best reasons to stay in Musquodoboit Harbour is to see and photograph the largest wintering population of Canada geese and black ducks on the Atlantic coast. A walking trail that follows the harbour past the lighthouse provides a superb view.

Rails-to-trails walkers cross an abandoned trestle at Musquodoboit Harbour.

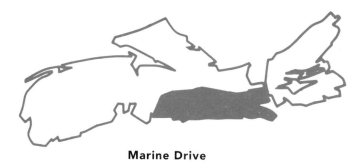

Marine Drive

Martinique Beach Hike: Spend a summer day walking on Martinique Beach, reachable by following signs off the Marine Drive about half a mile east of Musquodoboit Harbour. As the longest stretch of sand in Nova Scotia, at three miles, the beach is ideal for a brisk and worthwhile two-hour jaunt along the ocean.

Clam Harbour Beach Walk: Some 9.3 miles from Musquodoboit Harbour, off Route 7, is a road that leads to Clam Harbour Beach Provincial Park. Besides offering walkers a scenic, white sand beach with picnic areas and lifeguards, this facility has boardwalks and ramps for wheelchairs. Each year in mid-August, hundreds of people gather for the Clam Harbour Beach Sand Castle and Sculpture Contest. For hikers, there is a short hiking trail that mounts a hill behind the beach, affording excellent views of the coastline and offshore islands.

Taylor Head Hike: About 8.5 miles farther up the Marine Drive is the fishing village of Spry Bay. A dirt road that heads south leads halfway down the head, terminating at a parking lot and picnic area. From here, a boardwalk traverses delicate sand dunes and ends at a spectacular long beach, well suited for sunbathing. From the end of the beach, there are several excellent walking trails that meander to the end of the peninsula. The spruce, maple, and tamarack trees along the head have become stunted and gnarled from their intense exposure to wind, fog, and salt spray. Bird watchers will enjoy observing one of the province's largest cormorant colonies, which gathers just offshore.

Ship Harbour: The sheltered waters of Ship Harbour protect one of the world's largest aquacultural operations–"farms" that grow oysters and mussels. White marker buoys line the waters of the harbour, where an aquacultural centre is open weekdays from 9:00 a.m. to 5:00 p.m.

Sherbrooke: One should not leave the Marine Drive without visiting Sherbrooke, a restoration town on the St. Mary's River. The town was established as a fur trading post in 1655 and then settled 150 years later as a shipbuilding community. Much of Sherbrooke has been restored as it was in 1860. Costumed guides now lead visitors through the village.

1 2 GREAT BEACHES

1. **Evangeline Beach:** Near Avon River and Grand Pré; high tides, outstanding bird watching *(unsupervised)*
2. **Mavilette:** At Cape St. Mary, off Route 1, 32 km (20 mi.) north of Yarmouth; long coastal trail, excellent beachcombing *(unsupervised)*

SUNRISE TRAIL

3. **Pomquet:** In provincial park near Antigonish Harbour; two-mile beach, excellent swimming, lifeguards, good bird watching
4. **Melmerby:** Near Merigomish Harbour, 15.5 km (9.6 mi.) east of New Glasgow on Little Harbour Road; ocean beach on one side, warmer lagoon beach on the other; very popular

FLEUR-DE-LIS TRAIL

5. **Point Michaud:** 24 km (15 mi.) east of St. Peters Canal; two-mile beach, backed by marram-covered dunes, picnic area, hiking trail *(unsupervised)*
6. **Marble Head Mountain:** North of Dundee, on Bras d'Or Lake; spillage of marble chips make up this beautiful beach *(unsupervised)*

CABOT TRAIL

7. **Ingonish:** At entrance to Cape Breton Highlands National Park; freshwater and saltwater swimming; picnic area, clay tennis courts, baseball diamond, and soccer field
8. **Black Brook:** Picnic area and 10-minute walk through pine forest to Sqeekers Hole, a V-shaped formation in the cliffs, where tide rushes in

CEILIDH TRAIL

9. **Port Hood:** Approximately 46 km (28 mi.) from the Canso Causeway to Route 19 picnic area *(supervised swimming)*

MARINE DRIVE

10. **Clam Harbour:** On Clam Bay, south of Lake Charlotte; wide beach with salt marsh nearby; wheelchair accessible; site of sand-sculpturing competition every August (this year: August 15) *(supervised)*
11. **Taylor's Head:** Bull Beach at Taylor's Head provincial park; picnic area; one mile long; hard packed sand; large rock in centre of beach for climbing; hiking trail to lagoon
12. **Lawrencetown:** The surfer's beach! Best waves on the East Coast; 19 km (12 mi.) east of Dartmouth; change rooms, canteen

Cabot Trail

The 184-mile Cabot Trail is North America's most spectacular drive. Named for John Cabot, who landed on the island in 1497, this magnificent trail climbs, drops, and curves through virgin forests, around coastal headlands, and above sheer promontories.

Hikers who walk the highlands will be moved by the dramatic vistas and likely sightings of moose, whales, and bald eagles. But the views are only a part of what the Cabot Trail has to offer. The sights and sounds of Gaelic are alive on Cape Breton Island, waiting to be sampled and enjoyed.

Baddeck, one of Nova Scotia's premier resort towns, is the starting and ending point of the Cabot Trail. Located just off the Trans Canada Highway, the village sits on the shore of Bras d'Or Lake, an expansive saltwater inlet with 600 miles of alluring coastline. Many of its narrows become high fjords which host one of the world's largest populations of bald eagles. Its many harbours and coves attract yachters from all over Europe and the U.S.

It was in Baddeck that Alexander Graham Bell was inspired to build an estate and write that no place in the world compared to the beauty of Cape Breton Island. During the last 37 summers of his life, he conducted many successful airplane and hydrofoil experiments along its shores. Today Canada has created a national park and museum on the east end of town which features the inventor's many accomplishments.

Hiking near Baddeck can be as leisurely or challenging as you desire. Casual walkers can turn onto any of the mountain roads that crisscross the area and stroll for a mile or two past lookoffs,

For true highlands beauty, head for the Cabot
Trail, which winds along the perimeter of
Cape Breton Highlands National Park.

trout streams, and the Scottish farms that rim the town. In the late afternoon it is common to see white-tailed deer and even moose bounding across these walkways.

For trail hiking, Baddeck's most renowned path is Uisge Bann Falls Trail (pronounced ish-ga-ban) which features a 50-foot waterfall of unrivaled beauty.

Uisge Bann Falls Trail: After leaving Baddeck on Route 105, cross the bridge over the Trans Canada Highway and take the first right (marked for Uisge Bann Falls). Follow signs until the road forks, continuing right, and then watch for parking signs. A map of the trail is posted at the parking lot.

Uisge Bann is Gaelic for "white water," which is what awaits you about a mile up a moderately steep hill. The trail follows a brook through a dense forest of fir and birch trees. After emerging from a thicket of maples, the trail ends at a 50-foot waterfall that spills into a sunlit pool of crystal clear water.

From Baddeck, the Cabot Trail heads north to the highlands at Ingonish, 54 miles up the coast. For those traveling the Cabot Trail in this counterclockwise direction, a morning drive offers an awesome spectacle of coastal scenery, often bathed in warm sunlight. Binoculars and cameras should be kept handy as each bend offers another perspective on the rising coastline and occasional sightings of pilot whales, soaring eagles and hawks.

Just before reaching Ingonish,

the Cabot Trail climbs Cape Smokey, a 1,200-foot mountain, named for the white mist that often caps its peak. The highway escalates on consecutive hairpin turns with world-famous views. At the top of Smokey is a picnic park with spectacular views of the ocean and coastline. A three-mile hiking trail leads from the picnic area, looping through the rugged hillside.

From the summit of Cape Smokey, the Cabot Trail descends into South Bay Ingonish, where swimmers and walkers enjoy beaches along the quiet harbour. The eastern entrance of Cape Breton Highlands National Park is just beyond the waterfront.

Established in 1936, it is Atlantic Canada's first national park and sits at the heart of the Cabot Trail. There are two trails to consider hiking in this area, both within minutes of the entrance. The first, Middle Head, begins directly behind the elegant Keltic Lodge and the second, Franey Mountain, is a challenging uphill climb that offers outstanding highland views.

Middle Head Trail: To reach this 2.8-mile loop, follow signs to the Keltic Lodge passing the world renowned Highlands Links Golf Course. Beyond the links, the Keltic Lodge is perched on a raised cliff, surrounded by meticulously maintained gardens and views of mountains and ocean. Park behind the inn and walk to the signs indicating the start of the trail, which continues to the tip of Middle Head peninsula. Appropriately named, this narrow land formation sepa-

❧ Day Hiking Planner ❧

Franey Mountain

Length: 6.5 km (4 mi.) loop
Time: 3 to 4 hours
Degree of Difficulty: Moderate to strenuous
Special Features: Mountain climb with extensive views of river valley, the highlands plateau, and the ocean
Amenities: Parking lot with restrooms; posted maps
Entrance Point: Directly off Cabot Trail, 1.9 km(1.2 mi.) north of Highlands Park Visitor's Centre, follow signs to parking lot.

Franey's 1,000-foot ascent will test the legs and lungs of any who venture to its summit. The woods along the trail are extremely peaceful with only an occasional gust of wind stirring the top branches of the coniferous trees. Just beyond the halfway point, there is an excellent place to rest and enjoy a partial view of the valley below.

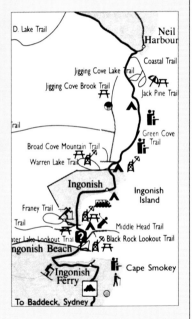

Franey Mountain is moose country. Keep your eye out for footprints and droppings. If you have an accidental encounter with these large but shy creatures, don't panic. Much like deer and even the rarer black bear, moose avoid humans whenever possible and, when met, quickly move on.

At the top of the trail, the woods open to stunning views of the sea and the Clyburn River Valley. Adventurous hikers can climb the 100-foot ladder to the fire tower on the summit, which offers an even greater perspective of the surrounding Highlands. Although Franey offers a different return route on a fire road, most hikers prefer to retrace their steps through the serene woods.

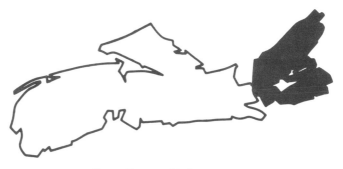

Cape Breton/Cabot Trail

rates Ingonish Bay into two almost equal halves.

The path is easily walked and has wide views of both bays, Cape Smokey, and Tern Rock, a sea stack where common terns nest during June and July. The tip of the trail ends high above the surf, which pounds the rock formations below. The hike up Middle Head trail is an excellent after- dinner trek, particularly as the sun sets over the Highlands.

DINGWALL AND POINTS NORTH

Fourteen miles north of Franey Mountain is the town of Dingwall. Along this section of the Cabot Trail are two very different hiking trails that typify the diversity of hiking in the Highlands. Both are well marked and easily accessible from the highway.

Warren Lake: The trail around Warren Lake is 5.3 miles long, fairly level, and smooth enough to jog. If you decide on an early morning walk, watch for moose and deer emerging from the woods, particularly at the western end of the lake.

Lake of Islands Trail: Plan a long day to undertake this ambitious trail which climbs from 300 feet to 1,250 feet, over eight rugged miles of bogs, open barrens, and forests. The hiking is strenuous and challenging, and the trail is often wet. The round trip is 16 miles, but the foray into the high plains wilderness is a satisfying challenge for ambitious hikers.

Dingwall, which lies outside the boundaries of the national park, has one of Cape Breton's finest sand beaches, ideal for walking, clamming or wading in the calm harbour waters. From the vantage point of the beach, the enormous headlands that encircle the harbour form one of the most scenic and captivating backdrops in Nova Scotia.

When touring the northern reaches of the province, hikers who wish to visit its least visited shore should leave the Cabot Trail at the town of Cape North and head to St. Margaret Village, Capstick, and finally Meat Cove. At this juncture, ambitious hikers can pick up a coastal trail to Red River, about 15 miles down the western coast. The unnamed trail, which begins where the road into Meat Cove ends, is impassable by motor vehicle.

Much of the trail hugs a high shoreline that is unpopulated and filled with wildlife. Although it can be walked in a long day, many hikers use backpacks and camp mid-route. One of the impediments of walking this trail is that hikers must make arrangements to be dropped off and met at Meat Cove and Red River, or retrace their steps.

Returning to the Cabot Trail at the village of Cape North, the highway passes along the mountainous plateau of the upper highlands to the turnoff for Lone Sheiling Trail. This half-mile loop is a dedicated pathway through 300-year-old sugar maples that tower over the forest floor, demonstrating what the primordial forests of Nova Scotia were once like. On the trail is a replica of a Scottish sheep crofter's hut, a memorial to the Scottish pioneers who settled the Cape Breton Highlands.

At Pleasant Bay, the Cabot Trail rejoins the coast at the Gulf of St. Lawrence where the highway's reputation for stirring vistas is world famous. For much of this century, the Cabot Trail along these mountains was an unbanked, dirt byway that was more challenging to drive than to walk. Today, thousands of visitors cruise its wide lanes which appear as a ribbon of concrete, snaking across the edge of the mountains with the sea just below. There are several outstanding walking trails along this section of Cape Breton Highlands National Park but none as sensational as the unique Skyline Trail.

Skyline Trail: From the heights of a headland cliff, this 4.3-mile loop overlooks the Cabot Trail and the variable waters of the Gulf of St. Lawrence. On calm summer days, pilot whales are often visible, breaching in small groups offshore. At the trail's highest vantage point of 1,350 feet, Skyline offers invigorating views of the looming coastline. In the afternoon, the setting sun is particularly photogenic as it sinks toward the Gulf of St. Lawrence.

Farther south lies Cheticamp (pop. 3,009), the largest town on Cape Breton's western shore. Boasting a distinctively French flavor, it offers many motels and inns, as well as the Acadian Museum, where artifacts of the area's first settlers are displayed. At the north end of town is the western entrance to Highlands National Park. All of its 27 designated trails are detailed in pamphlets available at the park offices. Hikers who plan to camp must purchase permits, also available at these sites.

Below Cheticamp, the Cabot Trail completes its loop by intersecting the Margaree Valley, which has become a popular destination for salmon anglers as well as hikers who enjoy hidden waterfalls, remote forests, and mountains.

Ceilidh Trail

A great wee ceilidh (pronounced *kay-lee*) is a Gaelic term for a stomping good time, which is the noted avocation of residents along this 67-mile stretch of Route 19. With Inverness on its northern end and towns like Mabou, Glendyer, and Creignish situated down its coast, these "Scotians" have preserved their Gaelic language and heritage with pride.

Musical events are planned throughout the year, featuring step dancing, fiddle music, and milling frolics (gatherings to soften freshly woven wool). The ocean is the prime resource of the people living on the Ceilidh, with fishing still anchoring the local economy. The coastline is rugged along the Mabou Highlands, where one of Cape Breton's best hikes can be found.

One of the features of the Ceilidh region are the many logging roads which leave the ocean to enter hill country. Most of these byways are waiting to be explored on foot. The people of the Mabou Highlands are especially friendly and are quick to answer a question or lend a hand. This kind of trekking should be unhurried and done in the spirit of adventure.

Sight Point Trail: This trail is marked by blue-gray circles as it follows the coast from a waterfall where stream and ocean meet, and then climbs the wall of a

Ceilidh Trail

Lighthouse at Mabou Mines marks Mabou Harbour.

rugged plateau. At times the path is very narrow and potentially dangerous as it crosses rock landslides on steep cliffs. Each section offers spectacular scenic views. There is a lyrical quality to the way the path alternates between open, exposed hillsides, and hidden glens of alder and fir. It is common to see whales playing in the sea and hear a symphony of songbirds.

Near the end of the walk, there is a marked lookoff which offers a fabulous view of ocean and farmland. This spot, overlooking Mabou Mines, is perfect for a picnic. Hiking boots and a windbreaker are necessary items to complete this exceptional hike.

❧ Day Hiking Planner ❧

Sight Point Trail

Length: 12.9 km (8 mi.) round trip
Time: 5 hours
Degree of Difficulty: Moderate to strenuous
Special Features: Outstanding views of the Northumberland Strait, farms, and river valleys
Amenities: None
Entrance Point: In Inverness, ask for location of Sight Point Road, then follow for 1.2 km (3/4 mi.). Look for blue signs on left, beginning the trail.

Fleur-de-Lis Trail

CANSO CAUSEWAY
TO LOUISBOURG

The Fleur-de-Lis Trail weaves along the Atlantic coastline, across southern Cape Breton Island, never far from the sea's many hidden beaches and strong surf. This is one of Nova Scotia's best spots for ocean treks while experiencing the historic Acadian culture. By exploring this region, hikers will appreciate a quiet but supremely beautiful part of Nova Scotia often overlooked by tourists.

The Fleur-de-Lis Trail starts at the Canso Causeway, which is the main thoroughfare between lower Nova Scotia and Cape Breton Island. By heading east to Port Hawkesbury, an established industrial centre, and proceeding past Cleveland into less populated Richmond County, you will reach open, relatively flat farmland that merges with the sea.

Where Route 206 joins Route 320, the town of Arichat appears, one of Nova Scotia's oldest communities with many restored shops and homes. From the edge of the harbour, the fishing fleet sits in front of the ocean in a particularly picturesque way.

Hikers will rejoice in opportunities to walk the coast just south of Arichat on the nearby island of Petit-de-Grat. It is the first of several outstanding treks that can be taken along the Fleur-de-Lis Trail, which follows the coast to the special town of Louisbourg.

From Arichat, follow the Fleur-de-Lis Trail northeast to St. Peters, where a fascinating canal is always busy with large and small craft shuttling between the Atlantic

A sunset cruise on Bras d'Or Lake provides a perfect ending to a day of "Active Living."

Fleur-de-Lis Trail

Ocean and Bras d'Or Lake. From St. Peters, follow the Trail (Route 247) for 15 miles to Point Michaud Provincial Park, which has parking and picnic tables, and offers hikers two excellent excursions.

Point Michaud: At low tide, Point Michaud Beach is flat and smooth, extending for almost two miles to a neck of land where rocks are occasionally occupied by seals. On a clear day, this round-trip hike of 4 to 5 miles is without obstacles, and nicely suited for fitness walkers. Because this area of Nova Scotia is sparsely populated and somewhat overlooked by tourists heading for the Highlands, there is a good chance that your hike will be solitary, particularly if undertaken on a weekday.

From Point Michaud, the Fleur-de-Lis Trail becomes a dirt road, passing the fishing town of L'Archeveque, which seems to be so unaffected by the commercial world that one doubts Hollywood could create a more picturesque maritime community. Beyond L'Archeveque, the still unpaved highway continues past the picturesque community of Forchu, to the village of Gabarus. At the end of the town, a dirt road bending right leads to a cemetery where the Gull Cove Trail begins.

Gabarus Gull Cove Trail: This trail begins at an old cart track that is a seven-mile loop through diverse landscape offering a quiet window on the bucolic life of eastern Cape Breton.

For the first mile and a half, the trail intersects mature woods which are less dense and scrubby than much of the woodlands in Cape Breton. Occasional streams and shallow ponds cross the path but can be easily negotiated. When the woods give way to an open field bordered by a stone fence, the ocean's striking coast appears. The trail follows the waterline for two miles, passing pastures with grazing livestock. At Cape Gabarus, you can climb the rocky cliffs for a fine view of Gabarus Bay.

The Fleur-de-Lis continues for 12 miles to the gateway of the Fortress of Louisbourg, which is one of Canada's most fascinating historic sites. From an interpretive centre across Louisbourg Harbour, visitors are bussed to the recreated 18th century settlement where a working community of soldiers and their families reenact the lifestyle of the period.

The fortress is the largest historical reconstruction in North America with a veritable village that includes residences, garrisons, an active bakery and eating house, and other functioning buildings required to operate a thriving community in the summer of 1744. One-hour walking tours are offered in French and English, and at the outskirt of the fortress, there are hiking trails that skirt the shore.

❧ Day Hiking Planner ❧

Petit-de-Grat Island Trail

Length: 14.5 km (9 mi.) loop
Time: 4 1/2 hours
Degree of Difficulty: Moderate
Special Features: Remarkable coastal views, highlighted by Green Island Lighthouse.
Amenities: Store in Petit-de-Grat, swimming along way
Entrance Point: Take Route 320, the main road of the Fleur-de-Lis Trail, toward the southernmost point, follow signs for Arichat on Isle Madame and then Petit-de-Grat. At end of village, road stops at parking lot. Start walk by passing last house on left and continue toward rocky shore.

On this ancient Acadian island, sheep paths lead away from the quaint fishing village of Petit-de-Grat, along beaches, numerous coves, and ponds. This ambling walk is long but, because it circles the whole island, it offers varied and dramatic views. Naturalists will appreciate the seals that sometimes appear along the rocks and pilot whales swimming in the surf.

Great blue herons hover along the water and sea gulls take turns dropping crabs and clams on the rocks.

At the halfway point you will find the Green Island Lighthouse, which marks one of the province's easternmost points. Be aware that the last part of this hikes passes over a beach. If the tides are high, you will need to wade through cold water. Time your walk to the tides or be prepared to go barefoot. At the fishing village of Sampson Cove, you will come to a small road which travels back in 1.5 miles to the parking lot in Petit-de-Grat.

Marconi Trail

A mere 37 miles long, the rugged Marconi Trail was named for the famous Italian inventor who established several "wireless" stations on its cliffs to broadcast radio waves to England. Along this eastern exposure, the power of the Atlantic Ocean is always present, beckoning walkers up its rocky cliffs, along coves and harbours.

Marconi Trail

The short Marconi Trail is blessed by the Main-à-Dieu Trail, a varied hike for walkers that boasts spectacular ocean views. The walk begins at Wild Cove, where the open Atlantic surf tosses tall plumes of foamy water on to the lower jut of land known as Cape Breton. A faint path floats uphill to cliffs, offering wonderful views of the rugged coastline, sheltered coves, and mossy, open moors. The scale and dramatic topography are magnified by the beauty and remoteness of this hike as it leads to the town of Main-à-Dieu.

It is possible to see harbour seals sprawled on the rocks of the shore and large seabirds circling curiously above them. About a mile from Main-à-Dieu, there is a delightful, broad beach suitable for swimming or soaking up the sun. Next, you'll see the town's lighthouse and, if it is misty, the deep fog horn at Moque Head will blast.

Main-à-Dieu has a general store and rest facilities. Take time to talk to the many generations of fishermen about working along this

Wander into the 18th century at Fortress of Louisbourg.

barely inhabited shore. After stocking up on snacks, retrace your steps across this beguiling, rocky land.

Other trails exist on the Marconi, most of which are explorations along the coastline. Hikers can walk south from Wild Cove, away from Main-à-Dieu, to the lighthouse at Louisbourg. This five-mile section of sheer cliffs and pounding surf is no less spectacular. To the north, where Homeville borders the Marconi Trail, a dirt road enters the jut of Cape Morien, which is an exposed and rugged landscape with informal trails that wind around the beach and rock precipices for about two miles. Nowhere in Cape Breton are walks more peaceful nor more connected to the power of the sea.

❧ Day Hiking Planner ❧

Main-à-Dieu Trail

Length: 12.9 km (8 mi.), round trip

Time: 5 hours

Degree of Difficulty: Moderate

Special Features: Swimming in coves, seals playing on rocks, remote and open moors

Amenities: General store, restroom at half-way point

Entrance Point: Beyond Louisbourg on Route 22, Marconi Trail hugs coast. After 5.7 km (3.5 mi.), look for dirt road on right, leading to ocean. Park at end, near small cairn.

Nova Scotia
BY REGION

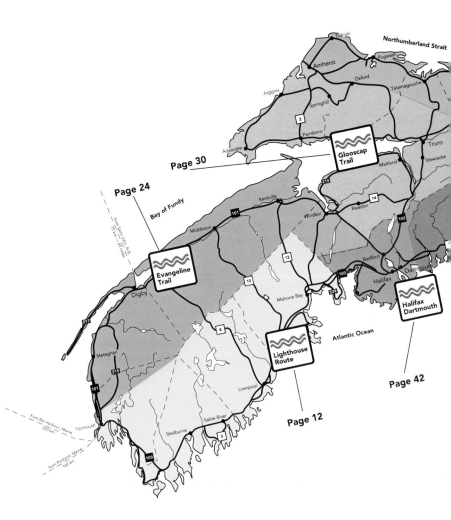

Northumberland Strait

Tidnish

Amherst

Pugwash

Oxford

Tatamagouche

Joggins

Springhill

Truro

2

Parrsboro

Stewiacke

Advocate

Page 30

Glooscap Trail

Maitland

215

Page 24

Bay of Fundy

Kentville

14

Rawdon

from Saint John, N.B.
75 km — 45 miles

101

Windsor

102

Middleton

Bedford

12

Dartmouth

Evangeline Trail

10

103

Halifax

329

Digby

Mahone Bay

Halifax Dartmouth

217

Atlantic Ocean

8

Meteghan

Page 42

215

Lighthouse Route

Liverpool

101

from Bar Harbour, Maine
320 km

Yarmouth

Sable River

Page 12

Shelburne

3

from Portland, Maine
160 km

103

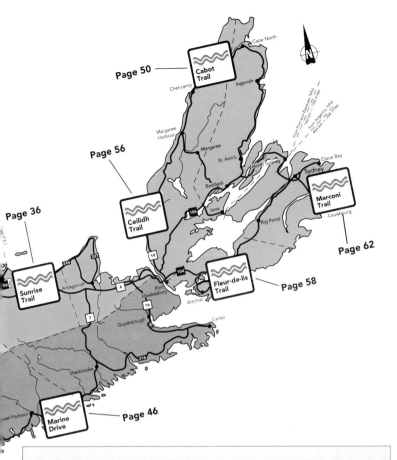

Page 50

Page 56

Page 36

Cabot
Trail

Marconi
Trail

Ceilidh
Trail

Page 62

Sunrise
Trail

Fleur-de-lis
Trail

Page 58

Marine
Drive

Page 46

NOVA SCOTIA FACTS & FIGURES

- Nova Scotia is a Latin name meaning *New Scotland*.
- Nova Scotia has the warmest salt water north of the Carolinas.
- Nova Scotia is 350 miles long but has over 4,600 miles of coastline
  — enough to stretch from Newfoundland to Los Angeles.
- Nova Scotia fishermen harvest 36 million pounds of lobster each year.
- Whale watchers in Nova Scotia can see eight varieties of whales,
  including the nearly extinct blue whale.
- With a population of just 888,000, the province hosts 1.5 million
  visitors annually.
- Nova Scotia has over a 100 sand beaches.
- Nova Scotia has more than 9,000 lakes and 100 rivers.
- Average summer daytime temperatures range between 66° F (18° C)
  and 75° F (24° C).
- The Bay of Fundy's 50-foot tides, are the highest in the world.

WHAT TO PACK
A NOVA SCOTIA HIKER'S CHECKLIST

Nova Scotia's weather is as diverse as its landscape. The warm currents of the Gulf Stream meet Arctic currents just off its shores, causing variable weather patterns. Spring, which is usually cool [2.5°C (35°F) to 3.9°C (48°F)], can be sunny and dry, or windy and wet. Summer grows mild, with highs of 24°C (75°F) and occasional rain storms; and autumn, with daytime temperatures of 16°C (50°F) to 18°C (65°F), tends to be clear and dry. Think seasonal when packing.

Here's a traveler's checklist, created with the walker/hiker in mind:

- Documents folder (passport or birth certificate required)
- Comfortable, waterproof hiking boots— a must for trails
- Wind jacket and pants
- Summer: loose-fitting walking shorts and tops
- Spring and fall: clothes for layering (low maintenance, high-performance garments made of poly-cotton blends and breathable fabrics like Gore-Tex) and wind-resistant outerwear
- Daypack with bug spray, bandanna, pocketknife, sunscreen, plastic poncho, compass, visor or brimmed hat, small flashlight with extra batteries, whistle and sunglasses
- Water bottle
- Binoculars
- Camera and plenty of film

A FEW HINTS ...

- In summer months, bugs are less attracted to light colored garments.
- Avoid bulky, heavier clothing. Spandex, layers of cotton, Gore-Tex, and even polypropylene materials will keep you dry and as cool or warm as you want. They are also quick drying and easy to hand wash.
- Walking sticks are invaluable for balance, safety, and upper body exercise.
- Less is better. Pack light.
- Causal wear is accepted in most of Nova Scotia's restaurants (however, jackets are required of men who dine at Keltic Lodge in Ingonish Beach).

10 GREAT BICYCLING AREAS

1. **Through the Annapolis Valley:** 100 miles, from Digby to Windsor, through rich farmland, apple orchards, gentle hills, views of Bay of Fundy

2. **Along the Sunrise Trail:** 129 miles along Northumberland Shore; full of seascapes, inviting side trips, dirt roads, great beaches

3. **Louisbourg to Point Michaud:** Dirt and paved roads, fishing villages, picturesque views, secluded beaches

4. **Anywhere Along the Cabot Trail:** Spectacular views, challenging hills

5. **Around Lake Ainslie:** Hilly inland area teeming with wildlife; two freshwater beaches between Inverness and Whycocomagh

6. **Yarmouth-Liverpool-Annapolis Royal Loop:** 100 miles along Lighthouse Route, through interior to historic Bay of Fundy area

7. **Bras d'Or Lake:** 600 miles of inland saltwater lake shore; little traffic on back roads; bald eagle habitat

8. **Along the Margaree River:** Along highlands and salmon river, past fields and forests, on west side of Cape Breton Island

9. **Cape Sable Figure Eight:** Site of Nova Scotia marathon on lower Lighthouse Route; fishing villages, seals, and other wildlife

10. **Digby to Brier Island:** Down Digby Neck, past fishing villages, to major birding island; ocean vistas; whale-watching cruises

Adventure Sampler

From bird-watching to sea kayaking, here's a sampling of more than 60 travel packages provided by Nova Scotia's hospitality and tourism industry. Listing is alphabetically by town, in six regions of the province. All prices are in Canadian dollars (taxes included in most cases).

HALIFAX-DARTMOUTH

Regal Tours
10 Akerley Blvd., Suite 55
Dartmouth, NS B3B 1J3
(800) 565-2777, (902) 468-8183, 864-8419; fax (902) 468-3704
Contact: Lauchie MacLean
Chauffeured limo & van tours; hourly, daily, multi-day sightseeing; Fossil Find on Glooscap Trail: $495 per person/ dble. occup. (3 days/2 nights, min. 4 people). Also: mushroom walks, farm stays, kayaking & cycling tours

Ambassatours Ltd.
1800 Argyle St., Suite 423
Halifax, NS B3J 3N8
(902) 420-9662; fax (902) 423-2143
Contact: Dennis Campbell
Moose, eagle, whale, and seal watching packages; plus salmon fishing and ranch adventures. Whale watching, $385 per person/ dble. occup. (2 nights, Jun.–Sept. 15); salmon fishing, $585 per person/ dble. occup. (2 nights, 8 people min., Jun. 1– Oct. 31)

Scott Tours
1707 Pryor St.
Halifax, NS B3H 4G7
(902) 423-5000
Contact: Wendy & Ron Scott
Three- and 5-day walking tours; exercise geared to your own pace, building to 10- 14 miles per day; picnics, candle-lit dinners, inns. Cape Breton Highlands National Park: $990 per person/dble. (5 days, meals, lodging)

EASTERN SHORE

(Marine Drive)

Salmon River House Country Inn
Salmon River Bridge, RR #2
Head of Jeddore, NS B0J 1P0
(902) 889-3353
Contact: Adrien & Norma Blanchette
Country inn, 6 rooms with baths. Canoe/portage to Jeddore Lake: $125 per person/dble. occup. (2 nights, meals, equipment)

Liscombe Lodge
Liscomb Mills, NS B0J 2A0
(902) 779-2307; fax (902) 779-2700
Contact: David M. Evans
Fishing, boating, tennis, quiet hikes; near Sherbrooke Village. Fishing: $450 per couple (2 nights, 4 meals, equipment & guide).

Wayward Goose Inn B&B
West Petpeswick Rd.
Musquodoboit Harbour, NS B0J 2L0
(902) 889-3654
Contact: Randy Skaling
  Quiet inn on 5 acres; private baths; swimming, canoe, daysailer, rowboat; trails, museums, craft shops, golf nearby. Golf Package: $209 for two (3 days/2 nights, 2 breakfasts, 2 lunches, 2 18-hole rounds)

Marquis of Dufferin Seaside Inn
RR #1, Port Dufferin, NS B0J 2R0
(902) 654-2696; fax (902) 654-2970
Contact: Michael & Eve Concannon
  Sail Away: $90 per person/dble. occup. (sailing offshore islands; 2 nights, 3 days; breakfasts; canoes & bicycles)

Salmon Lake Lodge & Sunset Cottages
RR #1, Sheet Harbour, NS B0J 3B0
(902) 885-2534; fax (same)
Contact: Bryan Lowe
  Seven cottages and lodge on lake; hike into Liscomb Game Sanctuary; fresh-and saltwater fishing. Packages: 1 to 6 days, $300 to $1,360 per person/dble. occup. (lodging, meals, equipment, guides & licenses; May, Jun. & Sept.)

Coastal Adventures
P.O. Box 77
Tangiers, NS B0J 3H0
(902) 772-2774
Contact: Scott Cunningham
  Sea kayaking and camping tours: 3 to 7 days, 4 to 6 participants, $200 to $875 (May to Oct.).

CAPE BRETON

(Cabot, Ceilidh, Fleur-de-Lis, Marconi Trails)

L'Auberge Acadienne
P.O. Box 59
Arichat, NS B0E 1A0
(902) 226-2200; fax (902) 226-1424
Contact: Beverly Boudreau
  19th century inn; 17 rooms with bath/shower. Packages for Fortress Louisbourg, Miner's Museum, biking, golf & kayaking. Hiking Isle Madame: $137 per person/dble. occup. (lodging, meals/picnics; May 1–Oct. 15)

Eagle's Perch B&B
P.O. Box 425
Baddeck, NS B0E 1B0
(902) 295-2640
Contact: Gail Holdner
  Variety of hiking, cycling, fishing, & canoeing packages; 11 km (6.8 mi.) from Uisge Bann Falls trails. Hiking: 1 to 3 nights, $27 to $73 per person/dble.

Four Directions Cape Breton
c/o Highwheeler Cafe
P.O. Box 719
Baddeck, NS B0E 1B0
(902) 295-3304
Contact: Daniel Atkins
  Adventures on foot: inn-to-inn, 5 days/4 nights, $849 per person/dble. occup.; guided trail tours, 1 day, $49 per person (with picnic; min. 3 people)

Inverary Inn Resort
P.O. Box 190
Baddeck, NS B0E 1B0
(800) 565-5660, (902) 295-3500; fax (902) 295-3527
Contact: Scott MacAulay, Angela Reid
  Lakeside resort, 137 bedrooms & cabins, restaurant, sauna, whirlpool, exercise equipment; open year-round. Outdoor Getaways: $122 to $332 per person/dble. occup. (lodging, meals, greens fees, boat tour of Bras d'Or Lake)

Mountain View by-the-Sea
Bird Island Tours
Big Bras d'Or, NS B0C 1B0
(902) 674-2384; fax (902) 674-2742
Contact: Joe & Mary Van Schaick
  Old home on Bras d'Or Lake; 3 B&B units with private bath; boat tours to nesting grounds of seabirds and seals (May 15 –Aug. 30); $110 per couple (2 nights, breakfast, 2 boat tickets)

Whale Works Enterprises, Ltd.
Whale Watch Bay St. Lawrence
Capstick, NS B0L 1E0
(902) 383-2981
Contact: Lori Cox
  Land and Sea Wilderness Weekends: sail on whale- and bird-watch one day, take guided wilderness trek the next; $204 per person/dble. occup. (2 nights/3 days, breakfasts & dinners, Jun. 15–Jul. 20, Aug. 20–Sept. 15).

Keltic Lodge
Middle Head Peninsula
Ingonish Beach, NS B0C 1L0
(902) 285-2880; fax (902) 285-2859
Contact: Alexander MacClure, John Hamilton

Resort on cliffs of Cabot Trail overlooking ocean; golf, swimming, tennis, nature trails; fresh- and saltwater beaches nearby. Golf Getaway: $293 per person/dble. occup. (2 nights, 2 breakfasts, 2 dinners, 2 days' greens fees, Jul.–Sept.; $234, Jun. & Oct.)

West Lake Ainslie Cottages & Outfitters
RR #3, Inverness, NS B0E 1N0
(902) 258-2654
Contact: Ray & Gwen MacFarlane

Housekeeping units overlooking lake with beach, dock, trout pond, walking trails, wildlife; excellent fishing; boat rentals. Vacation Adventure: $196.50 per person, $295 family of 4 (3 nights, plus trail ride, fly-fishing lesson, or Bird Island boat tour; Jun.–Oct.)

Highland Heights Inn
P.O. Box 19
Iona, NS B0A 1L0
(800) 565-5660, (902) 725-2360; fax (902) 725-2800
Contact: Bruce MacNeil

Small hotel in hills overlooking Bras d'Or Lake; hiking & mountain biking tours, eagle & whale-watching cruises. Eagles, Whales & Trails: $158 per person/dble. occup. (3 nights, 3 breakfasts, 1 picnic, outing, cruise & bike)

White Tail Lodge
General Delivery
Louisdale, NS B0E 1V0
(902) 345-2155
Contact: Blair & Vivian Sampson

Four cabins with bath/shower, refrigerator & stove; guides & equipment; fishing. Outdoor Special: $263 per person/dble. occup. (3 days/3 nights, dinners, guide, walks)

MacPuffin Motel & Inn
P.O. Box 558, Port Hawkesbury
Port Hastings, NS B0E 2V0
(902) 625-0621; fax (902) 625-1525

Outdoor Adventure: $139 per person/dble. occup. (3 nights, 2 box lunches; 2 1/2-hr. boat tour around Bird Island; Centennial Woodland Trails 3 miles away; indoor/outdoor pool)

Geddes Marketing & Development
P.O. Box 975
Sydney, NS B1P 6L4
(902) 562-0748
Contact: Trese MacInnis

Nelder's B&B in Big Pond (dry flower farm): 2-hr. nature walk, followed by folklorist ($60 dble.); 2-hr. walking tour, bird-watching, storytelling & jam-making ($88 dble.).

Dundee Resort & Marina
RR #2, West Bay, NS B0E 3K0
(902) 345-2649; fax (902) 345-2697
Contact: Graham Hudson

Resort overlooking Bras d'Or Lake, with marina and championship golf course. Golf Package: $216.25 per person/dble. occup. (3 nights, 1 bedroom cottage, 2 rounds of golf, dinner, canoe & box lunch, lake cruise, pools, trails; May 15–Jun. 30, Sept. 1–Oct. 15)

Kayak Cape Breton
RR #2, West Bay, NS B0E 3K0
(902) 535-3060

Three fully equipped two-bedroom cottages on Bras d'Or Lake; kayak tours & lessons. Kayak & Cottage Special: $530 for two (waterfront cottage for 1 week, free canoes, kayaks, or bikes; July–Aug.)

FUNDY/NORTHUMBERLAND
SHORES

(Glooscap & Sunrise Trails)

The Maple Inn
P.O. Box 457

17 Western Ave.
Parrsboro, NS B0M 1S0
(902) 254-3735
Contact: Bruce Boles, Lori Gilbert
Country inn with private baths; walk to shops & restaurants; 9-hole golf course 2 miles away; $109 for two (1 night, buffet breakfast, golf privileges)

Braeside Inn
P.O. Box 1810
80 Front St.
Pictou, NS B0K 1H0
(902) 485-5046; fax (902) 485-1701
Contact: Mike Emmett
Harbor views, 20 rooms, private baths; lunch & dinner daily. Summer Stay: $68 per person/dble. occup. (1 night, dinner, continental breakfast; maps for walking tours; day pass to rec. park; Jun.–Sept.).

Pictou Lodge
P.O. Box 1539
Pictou, NS B0K 1H0
(902) 485-4322; fax (902) 485-4945
Contact: Pat Ryan
Ocean Commotion Adventure: ride highest tides in world, 18 miles up tidal Shubenacadie River, with lunch on board; explore coastline of Cape Breton Highlands in search of whales; $279 per person/dble. occup. (4 nights, tidal bore rafting, 3-hr. whale-watching)

Train Station Inn
P.O. Box 67
Tatamagouche, NS B0K 1V0
(902) 657-3222
Contact: James Lefresne
Restored train station, 4 bedrooms with baths, dining room, laundry facilities, cafe. Harvest Fest: $59.95 per person/dble. occup. (1 night, breakfast, walking tour of rail line & berry fields; Aug. 15–Sept. 10)

EVANGELINE
TRAIL/ANNAPOLIS
VALLEY

Fundy Trail Farms B&B
RR #5, Berwick, NS B0P 1E0
(902) 538-9481
Contact: Derill & Marie Armstrong
Family farmhouse for 110 years, on North Mountain overlooking Bay of Fundy; (room for 4 couples. Weekend Getaways: $125 per person/dble. occup. (2 nights, 2 breakfasts, lunch, dinner, sleigh ride)

Brier Island Lodge & Restaurant
P.O. Box 1197
Brier Island, NS B0V 1H0
(902) 839-2300; fax (902) 839-2410
Contact: Ray Tudor
Lodge on bluff overlooking St. Mary's Bay and village of Westport; 10 rooms with bath/shower; home-style cooking; many hiking & nature trails; rockhounding. Cost: $165 per person/dble. occup. (1 night/2 days, 3 meals)

The Pines Resort Hotel
Shore Rd., P.O. Box 70
Digby, NS B0V 1A0
(902) 245-2511; fax (902) 245-6133
Contact: Brian Kloppenburg, Maurice Thiebaut
Recreation for all ages, including golf, tennis, swimming, and nature trails; whale-watching and fishing arranged; international cuisine. Golf Getaway: $155 per person/dble. occup.

The Olde 1980 Village Inn
Sandy Cove, 217W
Digby Neck, NS B0V 1A
(902) 834-2022
Victorian inn, quiet fishing village; walk to wharves & beaches for views of Fundy tides. Whale Watch: $205 dble. occup. (2 nights, breakfast for 2; vouchers for cruise; Jun., Sept. & Oct.)

Inn the Vineyard B&B
264 Old Post Rd., P.O. Box 66
(902) 542-9554
Grand Pré, NS B0P 1M0
Contact: John Halbrook, Cally Jordan
18th century home near Grand Pré Park; guided cycling through orchard country; river tubing option. $175 dble. (2 nights, 2 breakfasts, 2 cycling tours)

Down East Tours
Comp 41, RR #2
Kingston, NS B0P 1R0
(902) 765-8923
Contact: George Dagley
Walking/nature & cycling tours of Cabot Trail and rural Nova Scotia.

Cabot Trail Nature Tour: $1,080 per person/dble. occup. (5 nights, 5 dinners & breakfasts, guides, van from Sydney Airport; 5 days walking in Cape Breton Highlands National Park, plus visit to Bell museum in Baddeck).

Fairfield Farm Inn
10 Main St.
Middleton, NS B0S 1P0
(902) 825-6989
Contact: Shae Griffith
Country inn on 75-acre farm within walking distance to historic sites, museums & shopping. Annapolis Valley Adventure: $225 per couple (3 nights, breakfast, picnic for 2, museum passes)

The Planter's Barracks Country Inn
1468 Starr's Point Rd.
Port Williams, NS B0P 1T0
(902) 542-7878, fax (902) 542-4442
Contact: Jennie Sheito, Peter Mossman
Restored inn, 6 rooms with baths; tennis, barbeque. Nature Lovers Package: $178 dble. occup. (2 nights/3 days, 2 breakfasts, boxed lunch, hiking, bird-watching, or cycling)

Harbourview Inn
P.O. Box 39
Smith's Cove, NS B0S 1S0
(902) 245-5686
Contact: Mona & Philip Webb
Country inn, 10 rooms with baths; pool, tennis court, tidal beach. Lighthouse Harbour Tour Weekend: $139 per person/dble. occup. (2 nights, buffet breakfast, dinner for 2; cruise Annapolis Basin aboard *MV Sarah C*)

The Gallery B&B by-the-Sea
P.O. Box 719
Tiverton, NS B0V 1G0
(902) 839-2417; fax (same)
Contact: Tom Goodwin
Tour-boat whale-watching: $52 per person/dble. occup. (bikes & rods)

Ocean Explorations/Whale-Seabird Adventures
(Marine Explorations & Research)
P.O. Box 719
Tiverton, NS B0V 1G0
(902) 839-2417; fax (same)
Contact: Thomas Goodwin
Whales & seabirds cruises: $59 per person/dble. occup. (B&B, plus charter)

West Nova Nature Excursions
P.O. Box 147, RR #1
Weymouth, NS B0W 3T0
(902) 837-7172
Contact: Louis Gaudet
Hike, bike, fish, canoe the great Acadian forest and seashore. Shore Hike: $350 per person/dble. occup. (3 nights; 2 days canoeing, 1 day inland hiking, 1 day seashore hiking; 3 dinners, 2 breakfasts, 2 lunches).

Mountain Maple Lodge
RR #2, Wolfville, NS B0P 1X0
(902) 542-2658
Contact: Perry Munro
Log lodge plus lake outcamps & tent sites; home-cooked meals. Explore canals, bogs, and lakes by canoe: $245 per person (3 nights/2 days)

Old Orchard Inn
Greenwich, Exit 11, Route 101
P.O. Box 1090
Wolfville, NS B0P 1X0
(902) 542-5751; fax (902) 542-2276
Weekend Bike Tour: $245 per person/dble. occup. (2 nights, 2 dinners, 2 breakfasts, 2 box lunches; guided tour to Grand Pré National Historic Park, plus church and winery; bike rental $25 extra; min. 8 people)

SOUTH SHORE

(Lighthouse Route)

Freewheeling Adventures
RR # 1, Boutilier's Point, NS B0J 1G0
(902) 826-2437; fax (902) 826-7541
Contact: Cathy & Philip Guest
Van-supported bicycle trips; five-day packages in Annapolis Valley, Cabot Trail, and South Shore. South Shore Tour: $849 dble. (5 days/4 nights, lodging, all meals)

Chaslyn Tours
RR # 1, Haines Rd.
Bridgewater, NS B4V 2V9
(902) 543-6583
Contact: Lynn Murphy
Geological tours of Ovens Natural Park; cruises to seacaves & Blue Rocks. Lunenburg Walking Tour: $157

per person/dble. occup. (2 nights/1 day, meal coupons, Fisheries Museum)

South Shore Country Inn
Broad Cove, NS B0J 2H0
(902) 677-2042; fax (same)
Contact: Avril Betts
English country inn; two 2-bedroom units, 2 suites, dining room, near ocean & beach. Packages from $205 (3 nights, 5 meals) for bird & whale watching, ocean kayaking, cycling, tennis.

Loon Lake Outfitters
RR # 2, Caledonia, NS B0T 1B0
(902) 682-2220, 682-2290
Contact: Peter Rogers, Judy Flemming
Canoe trips in Kejimkujik National Park. 3-day package: $230 for 2 people (3 days canoeing; all camping equipment, food, canoe, camping fees, and shuttles; Jun.–Sept.)

The Whitman Inn
RR # 2, Caledonia, NS B0T 1B0
(902) 682-2226; fax (902) 682-3171
Contact: Nancy & Bruce Gurnham
Adventure Sampler: $449 per person/dble. occup. (2 nights in cottage, plus 2 nights in 2 inns; 6 picnic lunches, canoeing & hiking in national park, windsurfing & sea kayaking, ocean rafting; all equipment & instruction)

The Galley Restaurant & Lounge
P.O. Box 319
Chester, NS B0J 1J0
(902) 275-4700; fax (902) 275-2416
Contact: Ray Billard, Gail Fraser
Lodging at Mecklenburgh Inn. Golfing, hiking, fishing & water sports. Golf/Hiking: $389 per person/dble. occup. (2 nights/3 days, 2 dinners, 2 picnic lunches, ferry to Tancook Islands, mountain climb, 18 holes)

South Shore Trails Inc.
Clyde River, NS B0W 1RO
(902) 637-2167
Contact: Larry Fraser
Lodge on two canoeing rivers, near lakes, hiking trails, 9-hole golf course, and ocean beaches. 2-day canoeing, camping, horseback riding packages, from $200 per person (lodging, meals & equipment; guides available)

Manor Inn
Route #1, P.O. Box 56
Hebron, NS B0W 1X0
(902) 742-2487; fax (902) 742-8099
Contact: Terry Grandy
Country inn on Doctor's Lake, with tennis, canoeing, and restaurant. Whale Watch: $108 per person/dble. occup. (1 night, dinner, breakfast, excursion; Jun. 23–Sept. 21; $98 off-season)

Dauphinee Inn
167 Shore Club Rd.
P.O. Box 173
Hubbards, NS B0J 1T0
(902) 857-1790; fax (902) 857-9555
Contact: Rhys Harnish
Seaside inn, 4 rooms with baths, 2 suites; dining; hiking, boating, fishing, cycling. South Shore Adventure: $110 per person/dble. occup. (2 nights, 2 breakfasts, dinner; fees for Oak Island, Fisheries Museum & Tancook Island ferry; Jun. 1–Oct. 1)

Lane's Privateer Inn and B&B
27 Bristol Ave.
P.O. Box 509
Liverpool, NS B0T 1K0
(902) 354-3456; fax (902) 354-7220
Contact: Ron Lane
Inn has 27 rooms, B&B has 6; informal dining. Heritage/Ocean Tour: $103.95 per person/dble. occup. (1 night, dinner, breakfast; museum tour, deep-sea fishing)

Quarterdeck Restaurant & Cottages
Summerville Beach
P.O. Box 130
Liverpool, NS B0T 1K0
(902) 683-2998; winter (902) 354-3811
Contact: Doug Fraser, Frank MacIntosh
Housekeeping cottages on mile-long beach; whale watching, river/deep-sea fishing, canoeing & archaeology packages, from $360 for two (2 nights, picnic lunch, transportation, guide; minimum 2 people; May–Oct.)

Classic Inns of Lunenburg
c/o The Compass Rose Inn
15 King St.
Lunenburg, NS B0J 2C0
(902) 634-8509
Contact: Rodger Pike

Five 19th century inns offer cycling, fishing, whale-watching, diving & sailing packages, from $140 per person/dble. (2-3 nights, breakfasts, dinners, museum passes, equipment).

Jo's Dive Shop
296 Lincoln St.
Lunenburg, NS B0J 2C0
(902) 634-3443; fax (902) 634-9190
Full-service dive shop near Snug Harbour B&B. Two-day dive package: $120 per person/dble. with shared bath (1 night, breakfast, 1 boat dive per day for 2 days, equipment; min. 4 people)

Snug Harbour B&B
9 King St., Box 1390
Lunenburg, NS B0J 2C0
(902) 634-9146; fax (902) 634-3019
Contact: Nancy & David Callan
Package #1: $70 per person/dble. with shared bath (2 nights, breakfast, sailing on sloop or motor yacht, plus riding lesson or whale watching.

Bayview Pines Country Inn
RR # 2, Indian Point
Mahone Bay, NS B0J 2E0
(902) 624-9970
Contact: Curt, Nancy & Steve Norklun
Located on 21 acres; 9 rooms with baths. Sea Kayak Adventure: $160 per person/dble. occup. (2 nights, 2 breakfasts, box lunch, dinner; day of sea kayaking with guide; minimum 6 people)

Sea View B&B
P.O. Box 32
Port Mouton, NS B0T 1T0
(902) 683-2217; fax (902) 683-2216
Victorian home with 3 rooms, shared bath. Soft Adventure: $175 per couple/dble. occup. (2 nights/3 days)

Summerville Beach B & B and Country Chalets
RR #1, Port Mouton, NS B0T 1T0
(902) 683-2874
Contact: Alan Davis, June Lohnes
19th-century home & new housekeeping chalets on mile-long beach. Beachcombers Getaway: $179 for 2 in B&B, $279 for 2 in chalet (3 nights, picnic lunch, steamed mussels, choice of horseback trail ride, canoeing, or cycling; May, Jun. & Sept.)

The Ovens Natural Park
Outdoor Adventure Centre
P.O. Box 38
Riverport, NS B0J 2E0
(902) 766-4621
Housekeeping cottages & campsites on 200 oceanfront acres; ideal for kayakers, bicyclists, nature lovers, beachcombers & bird-watchers. Hiking, cycling, diving, sea-kayaking, whale-watching packages, from $119 (camp) and $289 (cottage) per person/dble. occup. (4 nights, self-guided itineraries, equipment)

J. Frank Jermey & Sons
RR #1 , South Brookfield, NS B0T 1Y0
(902) 682-3025; fax (902) 682-3112
Contact: Frank, John & Mike Jermey
Wilderness guide service; boating & canoeing for bird-watching, photography, sightseeing. Five-day canoe excursion: $75 per adult, $125 with guide

Spring Haven Canoe Outfitting
RR #3, Box 156
Tusket, NS B0W 3M0
(902) 648-0146
Contact: Larry Muise
Guided river trips, with all equipment & homemade foods; shuttle service from Yarmouth. Hourly ($20), day ($18 per person, 6-8 people) & overnight ($25/hr.). Picnic & Back-to-Nature Packages, $120 to $140 for 2.

White Point Beach Lodge Resort
White Point Beach, NS B0T 1G0
(800) 565-5068; fax (902) 354-7278
Contact: Doug Fawthrop
Resort on ocean beach with cottages & lodge rooms, dining room & lounge. Golf, tennis, swimming & boating. Beach Walk, Play & Golf Packages, $331.38 to $403.39 dble. occup. (3 days/2 nights, breakfasts, facilities)

Churchill Mansion Inn
RR #1, Yarmouth, NS B5A 4A5
(902) 649-2818
Contact: Connie Nicholl
Century-old mansion, 8 rooms with baths. Birding Package: $235 per couple/dble. occup. (2 days/2 nights, dinner, breakfasts, box lunch; 6-hr. tour)

SAMPLING
'A TASTE OF NOVA SCOTIA'

Hiking in the fresh air and open spaces of Nova Scotia makes a hearty appetite inevitable. First-time visitors are often surprised by the exquisite cuisine found in every part of the province.

Creative Nova Scotian chefs blend European cooking styles with local culinary traditions that date back to 1606, when, even in the wilderness of their outpost in Port Royal, Samuel de Champlain and his men prepared gourmet meals. Ever since, the prepared foods of Nova Scotia have raised the standards of fine dining for those who have sampled its myriad dishes that include lobster and scallops, salmon and trout, fresh seasonal vegetables, apples, and blueberries.

When seeking a place to dine in the province, look for an oval sign with the inscription "A Taste of Nova Scotia," indicating that the restaurant maintains particularly high food and service standards. Restaurants that display the seal have proven to a discriminating committee of food service and tourism experts that they serve meals using fresh, local ingredients, prepared with care, and served with genuine hospitality.

Member restaurants can be found throughout Nova Scotia. A list is available by writing: A Taste of Nova Scotia, P.O. Box 487, Halifax, NS B3J2R7. Please include a dollar for shipping and handling. The guide describes each establishment, average prices, hours, and credit cards accepted.

Nova Scotia Calendar

A Guide to Festivals and Events *

MAY

27-31   **Annapolis Valley Apple Blossom Festival**   *Windsor to Digby*
BBQs, sports events, art shows, coronation
ceremonies, parades, dances, concerts and
fireworks

29-30   **Cabot Trail Relay Race**   *Baddeck*
Running race around world-famous
Cabot Trail begins Saturday
morning; finishes 24 hours later.
Teams of 17 runners each.

JUNE

Walking tours of rocks, minerals, and   *Halifax County*
landforms of Peggy's Cove

Guardians of the Piping Plover: *Queens County*
Summerville Beach nature walks to learn
about natural history of special bird

4-6   **Shelburne County Lobster Festival**   *Shelburne County*
7th Annual celebration in "Lobster Capital
of Canada" includes lobster suppers,
sporting events, craft shows, boat races

11-13(T)   **Nova Scotia Forestry Exhibition**   *Windsor*
Exhibition highlights region's forestry
industry; includes logrolling show, etc.

13   **Natural History Walk**   *Halifax County*
Oakfield Provincial Park

18-20   **Celebration**   *Dartmouth*
Annual celebration of region's
multicultural community

18-20   **Uniacke Fire Fighters Fair**   *Mount Uniacke*

* **All dates subject to change; T = tentative**

JUNE

19(T)   **Salmon Supper**   *Caledonia*
Ox pull and planked salmon supper

19   **(through September 5)**
Lunenburg Dinner Theatre   *Lunenburg*
Tuesday-Sunday, 6:30 curtain:
four-course dinner and play,
"Bluenose on a Dime"

29-July 1   **Canada Day Ceilidh**   *Truro*
Musical entertainment, demonstrations,
concession stands

30   **(through September 26)**
Festival Antigonish   *Antigonish*
Live theatre; theatre for young audiences,
late night cabaret of Scottish concerts

JULY

Walking tours of historic Battery   *St. Peter's*
Provincial Park

Natural History of Blomidon   *Kings County*
Blomidon Provincial Park (7:00 p.m.):
interpretive walks through park
ecosystem

Guided tours of Shubenacadie Wildlife   *Colchester County*
Park (1:30-3:30 p.m.)

Summer Stage Theatre Festival   *Yarmouth*
Live theatre, musical entertainment,
arts and crafts exhibits

Concerts in Public Gardens   *Halifax*

Mid-July   **Five Islands Provincial Park** (2:00 p.m.):   *Colchester County*
rocks, minerals, and fossils of Bay of
Fundy; display and information on area's
geology

Hike & Smorgasbord Picnic   *Halifax County*
Dollar Lake Provincial Park (10:00 a.m.):
10K or 5K hike with Dartmouth Volksmarch
Hiking Club, followed by picnic

Beach Volleyball Tournament   *Yarmouth County*
Port Maitland Beach (12:30 p.m.)

Late July   Interpretive walking tours of rocks and   *Halifax County*
minerals of Peggy's Cove (7:00 p.m.)

JULY

Meet the Stars *Halifax County*
Dollar Lake Provincial Park (after
sunset): join amateur astronomers to
view various astronomical objects

Nature Feast *Shelburne County*
The Islands Provincial Park (9:00 a.m.to 2:00 p.m.)

1 Gathering of Clans & Fishermen's Regatta *Pugwash*
Scottish event features parade, lobster
dinner, highland games, dancing, pipe and
drum competitions, fireworks

1-4 Festival Acadien de Wedgeport *Wedgeport*
Acadian music and song, dancing, Acadian
food, Evangeline and Gabriel pageant

1-4 (T) Queens County Privateer Days *Liverpool*
Community festival based on historic
privateering days: recreations, privateer
feasts, auctions, competitions, etc.

1-7 (T) Nova Scotia International Tattoo *Halifax*
Spectacular production of music and
activities, with military bands from around
world, civilian dancers, gymnasts ,and choirs

1 (through September 5) (T)
The Ship's Company Theatre *Parrsboro*
Live theatre presentations aboard
historic *MV Kipawo* Ferry feature original
works performed by regional artists

2-4 Wolfville Centennial - Longfellow Days *Wolfville*
Concert, picnic and other events welcome
Americans to Wolfville during centennial year

3 Metropolitan Scottish Festival & Highland *Halifax*
Games
Scottish festival includes traditional
highland games, piping and drumming,
fiddling, highland dancing, and massed bands

4 American Visitor's Party *Halifax*
Town crier, Dixieland band, and refreshments
(7:30 p.m.)

4 American Visitor's Party *Bridgetown*
Royal Canadian Mounted Police noon
"capture" of tourists; ceremony, cake
cutting; American Tourist of the Year

JULY

July 6 **(through August 29)**
Chester Theatre Festival *Chester*
Tuesday-Sunday: summer theatre festival;
new show each week, plus special events

8-11 **Festival Acadien de Clare** *Clare*
Traditional and non-traditional activities
depict way of life of Acadian people

8-11 **Pictou Lobster Carnival** *Pictou*
Annual seaside festival, parade,
entertainment, boat races, fishermen
competitions, and marine exhibit

9-11 **Maritime Old Time Fiddling** *Dartmouth*
Contest & Jamboree
Top fiddlers from across North America
compete; final event features outdoor
variety show with group fiddling and
step dancing

9-11 **Judique on the Floor Days** *Judique*
Community events with Scottish flavour;
dances, concerts, parades, heavy weight
events, etc.

9-11 **Moosehead Grand Prix** (car race) *Halifax*

10 **Canning Country Fair** *Canning*
Celebrity cook-off, craft show, heritage
display, children and pet parades

10-11 **Festival of Quilts** *Clementsport*
Display at Upper Clements Park

10-11 **Lunenburg Craft Festival** *Lunenburg*
Highlights work of some of Nova Scotia's
finest craftspeople; community festival with
special dinners and entertainment

11-17 (T) **Big Pond Summer Festival** *Big Pond*
Week-long festival includes dances,
children's activities, strawberry festival.
Also 29th annual Big Pond concert: outdoor
Celtic music with best talent in Cape Breton

15-18 **Festival of the Tartans** *New Glasgow*
Highland dance, piping and drumming,
Scottish traditional activities; includes
track and field meet (July 16)

JULY

15-18	**Senior's Expo - "Life is What You Make It"** Consumer show for fiftysomething age group features entertainment, exhibits, seminars, arts, crafts and hobbies	*Halifax*
16-18	**Antigonish Highland Games** Highland dancing, pipe bands, piping competitions, heavy weight events, track and field athletics, ceilidhs, concerts, and tattoo	*Antigonish*
17	**Canada's Parks Day - Outdoor Recreation Festival and Second Annual Dollar Lake Triathlon** Dollar Lake Provincial Park: bird walks, plants walks, natural history walks, canoe rides and clinics, competitive events, and BBQ	*Halifax County*
17-25	**Atlantic Jazz Festival** Mainstage and late-night concerts; jazz concerts and jazz picnics each weekday	*Halifax*
17-25	**Seafest** Community event features parade, rumrunner and dory races, queen's pageant, and Great Nova Scotia Fish Feast	*Yarmouth*
22	**Midsummer Fan Fare at the Citadel** Mini tattoo, music, dancers, and performances by 78th Highlanders	*Halifax*
22-25	**Shelburne Founder's Days** Annual celebration of founding of town and its Loyalist heritage; variety of events	*Shelburne*
23-25	**22nd Annual Nova Scotia Bluegrass Oldtime Music Festival** Family event features acoustic country music, stage shows, field camping, children's activities, instrument workshops, etc.	*Ardoise*
23-25	**Glooscap Festival** Clams, outdoor jamboree, horseshoe tournament, fireworks	*Five Islands*
24	**100th Anniversary Bear River Cherry Carnival** Parade, auction, water sports, home-cooked meals, skydivers, fireworks	*Bear River*

Town crier announces
the happenings of the day.

JULY

25-31   **River John Festival Days**   *River John*
Features "North Shore Chowder Challenge"
on July 25: sample and voting on entries
in contest

26   **(through August 1) (T)**
South Shore Exhibition   *Bridgewater*
Major agricultural exhibition, home of
world's largest exhibition of oxen,
features international horse-and
ox-pulling competitions

28   **(through August 1) (T)**
Mahone Bay Wooden Boat Festival   *Mahone Bay*
Celebration of community-by-the-sea's
boat-building heritage features BBQs,
boat-building contest, exhibitions, etc.

30   **(through August 2)**
Atlantic Canada Bicycle Rally   *Yarmouth County*
Recreational bicycle event features
variety of town and social events

31 (T)   **Shriner's Field of Dreams**   *Baddeck*
Fiddle & Folk Festival
Fiddlers, step dancers, pianists, vocalists,
and highland pipers

31   **(through August 7)**
Action Week   *Sydney*
Annual community festival includes parade,
ball tournaments, picnic, street dance,
and concert

AUGUST

Walking tours of rocks, minerals, and   *Colchester County*
landforms of Five Islands Provincial Park
(1:30 p.m.)

Walking tours of the rocks, minerals, and   *Halifax County*
landforms of Peggy's Cove (7:00 p.m.)

Natural History at Blomidon   *Kings County*
Blomidon Provincial Park (7:00 p.m):
interpretative walks through park
ecosystem

Mid-August
Taylor Head Provincial Park (1:30 p.m.):   *Halifax County*
walking tours of rocks, minerals, and
landforms of Taylor Head

AUGUST
Late August

Shubenacadie Wild Life Park   *Colchester County*
Guided tours (1:30-3:30 p.m.)

Meet the Stars   *Halifax County*
Dollar Lake Provincial Park (after
sunset): join amateur astronomers to
view various astronomical objects

Night Insects   *Halifax County*
Porter's Lake Provincial Park: join
natural history expert to learn about
world of insects

1   **Nova Scotia Folk Art Festival**   *Lunenburg*
Annual showcase and sale of folk art by
more than 30 participating artists

1-8   **Digby Scallop Days**   *Digby*
Annual festival-by-the sea includes
flower show, musical entertainment, nature
walk, fish tub and sailboat races, scallop-
shucking, fish-filleting and net-mending
competitions

5-8   **The 55th Gaelic Mod**   *St. Ann's*
Competitions, concerts, and demonstrations
of Celtic arts and crafts

5-8   **Lunenburg Folk Harbour Festival**   *Lunenburg*
Top folk artists from U.S. and Canada
perform music in variety of locations

5-15   **Halifax International Buskerfest**   Halifax
International street performers:
food festival daily on waterfront

6-8   **Sam Slick Days**   *Windsor*
Street fair, children's costume parade,
grand parade, fireworks

8   **A Walk with Nature**   *Delaps Cove*
Guided walking tour (1:30 p.m.), BBQ and
refreshments (for all ages)

11-15   **Hector Festival**   *Pictou*
Scottish cultural festival features musical
entertainment commemorating landing of first
Scottish settlers aboard ship Hector fiddle-making

AUGUST

12-15 **20th Anniversary Festival of** *St. Ann's*
Scottish Fiddling
Evening ceilidhs followed by square dances,
workshops in fiddle, piano, step dance,

13-15 **Economy Clam Festival** *Economy*
Fiddle music, parade, dance, and jamboree;
plus clams fried, steamed, and in chowder

15 **Clam Harbour Beach Sand Castle** *Clam Harbour*
& Sculpture Contest
Registration (8:00 a.m.), competition (2:00 p.m.),
prizes awarded (4:00 p.m.)

19-22 (T) **Rock Hound Round-Up** *Parrsboro*
Gem and mineral displays, geological
tours and lectures

22 **6th Annual Chapin Bros.** *The Ovens Park*
Family Folk Concert

22 (T) **Feast of St. Louis** *Louisbourg*
Celebration of 18th century feast at
Fortress Louisbourg; music, dance,
cannon salutes, bonfires, and 18th
century fireworks

26-29 (T) **Nova Scotia Fisheries** *Lunenburg*
Exhibition & Fishermen's Reunion
Dory races, lobster trap making, scallop
shucking, grand parade, and Sunday
fishermen's picnic celebrate fishing
industry

28-29 **Yarmouth International Air Show** *Yarmouth Airport*

SEPTEMBER

3-6 (T) **Atlantic Fringe Festival** *Halifax*
40 shows/plays in eight venues

5 **(through October 10)**
Lunenburg Dinner Theatre *Lunenburg*
Tuesday-Sunday, 6:30 p.m. curtain:
Four-course dinner and play, "Bluenose
on a Dime"

9-19 **Amherst Four Fathers Festival** *Amherst*
Entertainment, quilt show and sale,
concerts, sports tournaments, parade,
and BBQs

SEPTEMBER

16-19   **Arts Festival X**   *Annapolis Royal*
              Film, performance and exhibits, costume
              arts, readings by famous Canadian authors

18   **Harvest Home**   *Baddeck*
              Alexander Graham Bell Museum event
              features picnic, harvest displays, kite-
              making, etc.

18   **Charter Day**   *Annapolis Royal*
              Special activities commemorate
              Nova Scotia Royal Charter of 1621

22-26   **South Shore Festival of the Arts**   *Lunenburg, Queens,*
              Visual and performing arts, crafts,   *Shelburne Counties*
              heritage and other cultural events
              throughout three counties; gala
              opening ceremony

23-26   **Bridgetown Ciderfest**   *Bridgetown*
              Variety of special events celebrates
              fall harvest season

24-25   **Oktoberfest**   *Tatamagouche*
              Traditional celebration of food and music

28   **(through October 2)**
              Oktoberfest in Lunenburg   *Lunenburg*
              Traditional food and music celebrate
              community's strong German heritage

Late September
              Annual Maitland Launch Day Festival   *Maitland*

Walking for Fitness

VIE ACTIVE MD
ACTIVE LIVING ®

There are several reasons why walking has become the exercise of the 1990's. It is, after all, an activity that can be pursued any time, anywhere, with anyone. Besides being fun, a walking regimen can be started easily at any age and can be worked into almost anybody's daily schedule—even when traveling.

Although some techniques are better than others, walking demands little skill or practice. It does require a pair of comfortable shoes, but no other specialized clothing or equipment is really necessary. And as long as you're in relatively good health, the activity presents few, if any, health hazards.

How well does walking stack up as a form of exercise? The answer depends on what you want from a fitness program—your goals for getting in shape and staying fit. Certainly, walking may not provide the same results as more strenuous activities. It won't, for example, tone or sculpt your muscles like strength and weight training will nor will it provide the same short-term aerobic benefits that, say, hill climbing or cross-country skiing will. But you may be surprised to discover how well walking does rank with other popular exercise activities and how beneficial it actually can be (see box, page 90).

Walking expends much energy. Striding at a brisk pace of 4 mph, for example, burns as much energy as bicycling at 10 mph. This makes it a very effective way to lose weight, since it burns fat away. An average (150-lb.) male will burn about 540 calories walking briskly up a 10% incline for 45 minutes. That's more calories than he would

A ramble through the hills of Annapolis Valley
(here near Hampton) exemplifies fitness walking.

One-Mile Walk Test

Minutes	MPH	Fitness Level
12 or less	5	Excellent
15	4	Good
17	3.5	Average
20	3	Fair
24 or more	2.5	Poor

burn if he were to run 5.5 mph for the same length of time.

Briskly walking up a 10% grade can be very strenuous. But even walking at a fitness pace of 4 mph on a level surface provides enough exercise to burn over 260 calories in 45 minutes. That's more than the average male would burn off cycling at 5.5 mph for the same amount of time. And the principle is the same for women, although on average they would burn 20% fewer calories.

So, how should you get started? Getting the most out of walking requires a few reasonable goals and a little self-assurance that walking for fitness is not only fun but can also be your answer to a lifetime of good health. One of the most important benefits of fitness walking comes from simply taking time off from the strains of everyday life. Universally, walkers report that their fitness programs help them deal with daily stresses. With few exceptions, they note, such exercise brings not only contentment but also clarity and focus to their thinking. Regardless of your age or fitness level, you can enjoy the same experience. Just set aside some time in the next day or so and take a walk. The following pointers will help you get maximum benefits from an activity that can reward you with a lifetime of fitness or, as we say in Nova Scotia, "Active Living."

1. Assess your current fitness level. Your goal should be to create a long-term plan that works—which means it must also be safe and enjoyable. Be realistic. If you are over 45, have been inactive, have a history of injury, or have a family history of heart disease, check with your doctor before pursuing a vigorous exercise program.

For a quick assessment of your overall conditioning, try the one-mile walk test (use landmarks or a school track).

Two rules of thumb for a walking workout: 1. You should be able to carry on a normal conversation while walking; if you're out of breath, slow down—you're overdoing it; 2. If you can't comfortably repeat the same distance at the same pace the next day, give yourself a break—you're walking too far, too fast, too soon.

2. Find your target heart rate. Monitor your heart rate to ensure best—and safest—results. Your walking workouts or other exercise activity should be intense enough to raise your heart rate to 60% to 80% of your maximum heart rate (MHR). To determine this target range, first subtract your age from 220 (beats per minute). This is your MHR. Then, multiply your MHR by .6 and .8 to establish your target heart rate (THR) range. If you are 45, for example, your THR would range from 105 to 140 beats per

12-Week Starter Plan

Week	Pace (min./mi.)	(mph)	Distance (mi.)	Time (min.)	Frequency (days/wk.)
1	24	2.5	3/4	18	3
2	24	2.5	1	24	3
3-4	20	3.0	1 1/2	30	3
5-6	20	3.0	2	40	4
7-8	20	3.0	2 1/2	50	4
9-10	18 1/2	3.25	3	55	5
11-12	17	3.5	3 1/2	60	5

minute (220 - 45 = 175 x .6 and .8).

If you are just beginning a fitness program, you should exercise at 60% of your maximum heart rate. At moderate and advanced levels, move up to 70% and 80%, respectively. The Traveler's Training Log (see page 92) is geared to 70% to 75% of MHR.

3. Set up a 12-week starter plan. To begin an exercise walking program, focus on time, not distance. Start with 18- to 20-minute walks three days a week for the first few weeks. Increase your time as you feel comfortable. Exercise at 60% of your MHR for the first few weeks, moving up to 70% to 75% gradually. As you become fitter, you'll have to stride faster to reach that THR. Build your pace comfortably. As your speed picks up, your stride will lengthen and so will your distance. Your goal should be to walk at least five times a week, at 3.5 to 4 mph, for 45 to 60 minutes. At that rate, you will burn approximately 300 to 400 calories an hour. You'll also be covering about 17 miles (27 km) per week—an ideal distance for building trail conditioning and travel endurance.

4. Stick with it. Don't be a dropout. When it comes to success, studies show higher rates of adherence to walking than to any other exercise program. Still, dropout rates range from 25% to 50%. How can you avoid becoming a statistic and assure that your fitness plan becomes a long-term proposition? Here are five pointers to help you overcome the obstacles that many walkers encounter:

a. Set goals and reward yourself. Pick a minimum distance you'll walk: two miles, 30 minutes, 20 telephone poles. When you reach your goal, pat yourself on the back. Think of other fun things you like to do (call a friend, read a book, see a movie)—and don't do them until you've walked. Or walk to where you'll meet a friend or go to the movies. Keep a positive attitude—don't wake up asking yourself *if* you'll walk today, but *when* you'll walk. Such goals are elementary, but they can make a difference until you get hooked and walking becomes its own reward.

b. *Beat boredom*. One of the greatest enemies of exercise is boredom—the monotony of the same old routine. The solution is simply variety: different companion(s), new routes, other times, or simple games. Walk up hills or stairs (be ready for a more vigorous workout, however). Try different speeds. Take a turn on your high school track, *backwards*. Anything that will break the tedium will keep you going and make your walking fun.

c. *Walk with a friend*. Spouse, partner, neighbor, or fellow worker—it doesn't matter. A walking companion not only makes the activity social and more fun, it gives you a commitment to another person—a strong motivator.

d. *Join a club*. Community centers, health clubs, hospitals, and shopping malls are forming walk-

---

BALANCING ACT

For well-rounded fitness, blend physical activities that you enjoy into a balanced program that combines fitness walking with other low-impact aerobic exercises—cycling, swimming, or canoeing/kayaking.

All four activities are easily accessible in Nova Scotia and all are excellent for weight loss and development of aerobic capacity. Each, however, has benefits and drawbacks from a "training" standpoint:

Fitness walking—*Benefits:* strengthens heart and legs; aids breathing; excellent stress reliever; low injury potential; minimal equipment needs (sturdy shoes); no special skills required; easily becomes a "life sport." *Drawbacks:* does little to build upper body (proper arm swing helps, but weights or striding poles are required for serious upper body workouts).

Cycling—*Benefits:* excellent for strengthening and toning leg muscles; firms up buttocks faster than walking; minimal impact on bones and joints (although it puts more demands on hips and knees than walking). *Drawbacks:* does little to build upper body; can create tension in back, shoulders, and neck.

Swimming—*Benefits:* exercises all major muscle groups; buoyancy minimizes impact on bones and joints; builds overall endurance; excellent stress reliever; can become a "life sport." *Drawbacks:* does little to strengthen bones; requires special skills.

Canoeing/kayaking—*Benefits:* excellent for building upper body; strengthens abdominal, arm, shoulder, and back muscles; good stress reliever. Drawbacks: little or no benefit to leg muscles; requires special skills.

How Far, How Fast?

A realistic goal for fitness walking as exercise is to cover at least two miles (3.2 km) in 30 minutes (that's 15 minutes per mile, or 4 mph). For most walkers over 40 years old, this pace will raise the heart rate to 120 to 125 beats per minute—an appropriate level for sound cardiovascular health. Walking two miles (3.2 km) in 30 minutes also results in a workout (and caloric burn) equal to aerobics or jogging for about 20 minutes.

To determine your speed, find the total time of your walk in the left-hand column. Then, move across to the column indicating the distance of your walk. The figure in the box is your speed in miles per hour. Example, if you walk four miles in 80 minutes, your speed is 3 mph. (To convert to kilometers, divide miles by .62.)

Time (minutes)	Distance (miles)							
	1	**2**	**3**	**4**	**5**	**6**	**7**	**8**
20	3.0	6.0	9.0	12.0	15.0	18.0	21.0	24.0
40	1.5	3.0	4.5	6.0	7.5	9.0	10.5	12.0
60	1.0	2.0	3.0	4.0	5.0	6.0	7.0	8.0
80	0.8	1.5	2.3	3.0	3.8	4.5	5.3	6.0
100	0.6	1.2	1.8	2.4	3.0	3.6	4.2	4.8
120	0.5	1.0	1.5	2.0	2.5	3.0	3.5	4.0

ing clubs to promote the activity's benefits and enjoyment. Besides the opportunity to meet new friends, membership generally offers everything from health clinics to organized walking events.

e. Record your progress. Keep a log (see pages 92–126). Once you've started a walking program, keep track of your mileage, time, heart rate, and, perhaps, even feelings about yourself. Jotting down progress is motivational; it's also rewarding to watch your distance and speed go up while your weight, waistline, and heart rate go down. The log will also become an enjoyable diary for looking back on both a personal achievement and your Nova Scotia walking vacation.

Nova Scotia Walker's Log

T ravel vacations should be as exhilarating as they are relaxing. To get the most out of your Nova Scotia holidays, make conditioning part of your travel planning.

A "training" regimen geared to walking and hiking will help you tone your muscles, lose weight, and boost your aerobic capacity. But the real bottom line—for your Nova Scotia getaway—will be improved endurance and enhanced enjoyment of the Walker's Province.

This log is designed as a 26-week program for fitness before, during, and after your trip. It begins with a 12-week buildup for an active vacation that includes day hikes ranging from 3 km (2 mi.) to 21 km (13 mi.). It also features a diary (see pages108-111) for recording your activities during your Nova Scotia visit, and a 12-week post-trip record to keep you on the route to a lifetime of fitness.

Set a goal for each week, increasing your activity gradually. If you have been sedentary, start slowly— say, a mile or so three times a week for the first two or three weeks. By the 10th or 12th week, you should be covering 26 km (16 mi.)to 32 km (20 mi.) comfortably.

To help keep your program balanced, be sure to record other physical activities—sports (e.g., tennis, racquetball, basketball); any other low impact exercise (swimming, cycling, cross-country skiing); use of indoor exercise equipment; and special chores, such as chopping wood, shoveling snow, mowing, or raking. Aim for at least two or three hours per week.

Note: The pulse check is a quick method for making sure that your level of exercise is appropriate. After about 20 minutes of walking, you should reach 70% to 75% of your maximum heart rate (MHR = 220 minus your age). To take your pulse, pause and place two fingers on the side of your neck until you feel the beat. Count the beats for 15 seconds, then multiply by four. That's your target heart rate.

If you're 40 years old, for example, your target rate should be 126 to 135 (220 - 40 = 180 x .70 and .75). If your pulse is lower than your target, pick up your pace or climb a few steps or hills; if it is higher than your target range, slow down or take a less demanding route.

Traveler's Training Log

Week _____ **Goal (Time/Distance)** _____ / _____

Day	Walking/Hiking Routes & Notes	Pulse Check*	Time hrs./min.	Distance (miles)
Mon.				
Tues.				
Wed.				
Thurs.				
Fri.				
Sat.				
Sun.				

* Heart rate after 20 minutes of walking/hiking

Weekly Totals

Other Activities

		Time hrs./min.
Mon.		
Tues.		
Wed.		
Thurs.		
Fri.		
Sat.		
Sun.		
	Weekly Total	

Traveler's Training Log

Week _____ **Goal (Time/Distance)** _____ **/** _____

Day	Walking/Hiking Routes & Notes	Pulse Check*	Time hrs./min.	Distance (miles)
Mon.				
Tues.				
Wed.				
Thurs.				
Fri.				
Sat.				
Sun.				

* Heart rate after 20 minutes of walking/hiking

Weekly Totals

Other Activities

Time hrs./min.

Day		Time hrs./min.
Mon.		
Tues.		
Wed.		
Thurs.		
Fri.		
Sat.		
Sun.		
	Weekly Total	

Traveler's Training Log

Week _____   **Goal (Time/Distance)** _____ / _____

Day	Walking/Hiking Routes & Notes	Pulse Check*	Time hrs./min.	Distance (miles)
Mon.				
Tues.				
Wed.				
Thurs.				
Fri.				
Sat.				
Sun.				
* Heart rate after 20 minutes of walking/hiking		**Weekly Totals**		

Other Activities

Day		Time hrs./min.
Mon.		
Tues.		
Wed.		
Thurs.		
Fri.		
Sat.		
Sun.		
	Weekly Total	

Traveler's Training Log

Week _____ **Goal (Time/Distance)** _____ **/** _____

Day	Walking/Hiking Routes & Notes	Pulse Check*	Time hrs./min.	Distance (miles)
Mon.				
Tues.				
Wed.				
Thurs.				
Fri.				
Sat.				
Sun.				

* Heart rate after 20 minutes of walking/hiking

Weekly Totals

Other Activities

		Time hrs./min.
Mon.		
Tues.		
Wed.		
Thurs.		
Fri.		
Sat.		
Sun.		
	Weekly Total	

Early fall inspires a sidetrip through an orchard in Upper Canard on the Evangeline Trail.

Traveler's Training Log

Week _____ **Goal (Time/Distance)** _____ **/** _____

Day	Walking/Hiking Routes & Notes	Pulse Check*	Time hrs./min.	Distance (miles)
Mon.				
Tues.				
Wed.				
Thurs.				
Fri.				
Sat.				
Sun.				
* Heart rate after 20 minutes of walking/hiking **Weekly Totals**				

Other Activities

		Time hrs./min.
Mon.		
Tues.		
Wed.		
Thurs.		
Fri.		
Sat.		
Sun.		
	Weekly Total	

Traveler's Training Log

Week _____ **Goal (Time/Distance)** _____ / _____

Day	Walking/Hiking Routes & Notes	Pulse Check*	Time hrs./min.	Distance (miles)
Mon.				
Tues.				
Wed.				
Thurs.				
Fri.				
Sat.				
Sun.				
* Heart rate after 20 minutes of walking/hiking		**Weekly Totals**		

Other Activities

		Time hrs./min.
Mon.		
Tues.		
Wed.		
Thurs.		
Fri.		
Sat.		
Sun.		
	Weekly Total	

Traveler's Training Log

Week _____ **Goal (Time/Distance)** _____ **/** _____

Day	Walking/Hiking Routes & Notes	Pulse Check*	Time hrs./min.	Distance (miles)
Mon.				
Tues.				
Wed.				
Thurs.				
Fri.				
Sat.				
Sun.				

* Heart rate after 20 minutes of walking/hiking

Weekly Totals

Other Activities

		Time hrs./min.
Mon.		
Tues.		
Wed.		
Thurs.		
Fri.		
Sat.		
Sun.		
	Weekly Total	

Traveler's Training Log

Week _____   **Goal (Time/Distance)** _____ **/** _____

Day	Walking/Hiking Routes & Notes	Pulse Check*	Time hrs./min.	Distance (miles)
Mon.				
Tues.				
Wed.				
Thurs.				
Fri.				
Sat.				
Sun.				

* Heart rate after 20 minutes of walking/hiking

Weekly Totals

Other Activities

		Time hrs./min.
Mon.		
Tues.		
Wed.		
Thurs.		
Fri.		
Sat.		
Sun.		
	Weekly Total	

From bold headlands to huge sandy beaches,
Nova Scotia challenges hikers and rockhounders alike.

Traveler's Training Log

Week _____   Goal (Time/Distance) _____ / _____

Day	Walking/Hiking Routes & Notes	Pulse Check*	Time hrs./min.	Distance (miles)
Mon.				
Tues.				
Wed.				
Thurs.				
Fri.				
Sat.				
Sun.				
* Heart rate after 20 minutes of walking/hiking **Weekly Totals**				

Other Activities

Day		Time hrs./min.
Mon.		
Tues.		
Wed.		
Thurs.		
Fri.		
Sat.		
Sun.		
	Weekly Total	

Traveler's Training Log

Week _____ **Goal (Time/Distance)** _____ **/** _____

Day	Walking/Hiking Routes & Notes	Pulse Check*	Time hrs./min.	Distance (miles)
Mon.				
Tues.				
Wed.				
Thurs.				
Fri.				
Sat.				
Sun.				
* Heart rate after 20 minutes of walking/hiking		**Weekly Totals**		

Other Activities

		Time hrs./min.
Mon.		
Tues.		
Wed.		
Thurs.		
Fri.		
Sat.		
Sun.		
	Weekly Total	

Traveler's Training Log

Week _____ **Goal (Time/Distance)** _____ / _____

Day	Walking/Hiking Routes & Notes	Pulse Check*	Time hrs./min.	Distance (miles)
Mon.				
Tues.				
Wed.				
Thurs.				
Fri.				
Sat.				
Sun.				
* Heart rate after 20 minutes of walking/hiking **Weekly Totals**				

Other Activities

		Time hrs./min.
Mon.		
Tues.		
Wed.		
Thurs.		
Fri.		
Sat.		
Sun.		
	Weekly Total	

Traveler's Training Log

Week _____   Goal (Time/Distance) _____ / _____

Day	Walking/Hiking Routes & Notes	Pulse Check*	Time hrs./min.	Distance (miles)
Mon.				
Tues.				
Wed.				
Thurs.				
Fri.				
Sat.				
Sun.				
* Heart rate after 20 minutes of walking/hiking **Weekly Totals**				

Other Activities

Day	Activity	Time hrs./min.
Mon.		
Tues.		
Wed.		
Thurs.		
Fri.		
Sat.		
Sun.		
	Weekly Total	

Stroll through history at Grand Pré, site of an Acadian village and scene for Longfellow's "Evangeline."

Nova Scotia Traveler's Log

Week _____

Day	Time of day	Walking/Hiking Routes & Trails	Terrain & Features
1			
2			
3			
4			
5			
6			
7			

Nova Scotia Trip Log

Day	Date	Starting Pt.	Finish Pt.	Highways/Routes
1				
2				
3				
4				
5				
6				
7				

Duration (hrs./min.)	Distance (km or mi.)	Highlights	Day
			1
			2
			3
			4
			5
			6
			7

Lodging	Memorable Attractions	Activities	Day
			1
			2
			3
			4
			5
			6
			7

Nova Scotia Traveler's Log

Week _____

Day	Time of day	Walking/Hiking Routes & Trails	Terrain & Features
8			
9			
10			
11			
12			
13			
14			

Nova Scotia Trip Log

Day	Date	Starting Pt.	Finish Pt.	Highways/Routes
8				
9				
10				
11				
12				
13				
14				

Duration (hrs./min.)	Distance (km or mi.)	Highlights	Day
			8
			9
			10
			11
			12
			13
			14

Lodging	Memorable Attractions	Activities	Day
			8
			9
			10
			11
			12
			13
			14

How many ways are there to define *serenity*?
Count the number of seaside villages in Nova Scotia.

Traveler's Training Log

Week _____ **Goal (Time/Distance)** _____ **/** _____

Day	Walking/Hiking Routes & Notes	Pulse Check*	Time hrs./min.	Distance (miles)
Mon.				
Tues.				
Wed.				
Thurs.				
Fri.				
Sat.				
Sun.				
* Heart rate after 20 minutes of walking/hiking	**Weekly Totals**			

Other Activities

Day		Time hrs./min.
Mon.		
Tues.		
Wed.		
Thurs.		
Fri.		
Sat.		
Sun.		
	Weekly Total	

Traveler's Training Log

Week _____ **Goal (Time/Distance)** _____ / _____

Day	Walking/Hiking Routes & Notes	Pulse Check*	Time hrs./min.	Distance (miles)
Mon.				
Tues.				
Wed.				
Thurs.				
Fri.				
Sat.				
Sun.				
* Heart rate after 20 minutes of walking/hiking	**Weekly Totals**			

Other Activities

		Time hrs./min.
Mon.		
Tues.		
Wed.		
Thurs.		
Fri.		
Sat.		
Sun.		
	Weekly Total	

Traveler's Training Log

Week _____   Goal (Time/Distance) _____ / _____

Day	Walking/Hiking Routes & Notes	Pulse Check*	Time hrs./min.	Distance (miles)
Mon.				
Tues.				
Wed.				
Thurs.				
Fri.				
Sat.				
Sun.				

* Heart rate after 20 minutes of walking/hiking

Weekly Totals

Other Activities

Day		Time hrs./min.
Mon.		
Tues.		
Wed.		
Thurs.		
Fri.		
Sat.		
Sun.		
	Weekly Total	

Traveler's Training Log

Week _____   **Goal (Time/Distance)** _____ / _____

Day	Walking/Hiking Routes & Notes	Pulse Check*	Time hrs./min.	Distance (miles)
Mon.				
Tues.				
Wed.				
Thurs.				
Fri.				
Sat.				
Sun.				
* Heart rate after 20 minutes of walking/hiking		**Weekly Totals**		

Other Activities

Day		Time hrs./min.
Mon.		
Tues.		
Wed.		
Thurs.		
Fri.		
Sat.		
Sun.		
	Weekly Total	

These vacationers add Sanford, a fishing village near Yarmouth, to their list of "impulse" walks.

Traveler's Training Log

Week _____ **Goal (Time/Distance)** _____ / _____

Day	Walking/Hiking Routes & Notes	Pulse Check*	Time hrs./min.	Distance (miles)
Mon.				
Tues.				
Wed.				
Thurs.				
Fri.				
Sat.				
Sun.				
* Heart rate after 20 minutes of walking/hiking		**Weekly Totals**		

Other Activities

Day		Time hrs./min.
Mon.		
Tues.		
Wed.		
Thurs.		
Fri.		
Sat.		
Sun.		
	Weekly Total	

Traveler's Training Log

Week _____ **Goal (Time/Distance)** _____ **/** _____

Day	Walking/Hiking Routes & Notes	Pulse Check*	Time hrs./min.	Distance (miles)
Mon.				
Tues.				
Wed.				
Thurs.				
Fri.				
Sat.				
Sun.				
* Heart rate after 20 minutes of walking/hiking **Weekly Totals**				

Other Activities

Day		Time hrs./min.
Mon.		
Tues.		
Wed.		
Thurs.		
Fri.		
Sat.		
Sun.		
	Weekly Total	

Traveler's Training Log

Week _____ **Goal (Time/Distance)** _____ / _____

Day	Walking/Hiking Routes & Notes	Pulse Check*	Time hrs./min.	Distance (miles)
Mon.				
Tues.				
Wed.				
Thurs.				
Fri.				
Sat.				
Sun.				

* Heart rate after 20 minutes of walking/hiking

Weekly Totals

Other Activities

		Time hrs./min.
Mon.		
Tues.		
Wed.		
Thurs.		
Fri.		
Sat.		
Sun.		
	Weekly Total	

Traveler's Training Log

Week _____ **Goal (Time/Distance)** _____ / _____

Day	Walking/Hiking Routes & Notes	Pulse Check*	Time hrs./min.	Distance (miles)
Mon.				
Tues.				
Wed.				
Thurs.				
Fri.				
Sat.				
Sun.				

* Heart rate after 20 minutes of walking/hiking

Weekly Totals

Other Activities

		Time hrs./min.
Mon.		
Tues.		
Wed.		
Thurs.		
Fri.		
Sat.		
Sun.		
	Weekly Total	

It's time to take a snapshot during a trek along
the Margaree River, off the Cabot Trail.

Traveler's Training Log

Week _____ **Goal (Time/Distance)** _____ / _____

Day	Walking/Hiking Routes & Notes	Pulse Check*	Time hrs./min.	Distance (miles)
Mon.				
Tues.				
Wed.				
Thurs.				
Fri.				
Sat.				
Sun.				

* Heart rate after 20 minutes of walking/hiking

Weekly Totals

Other Activities

Day		Time hrs./min.
Mon.		
Tues.		
Wed.		
Thurs.		
Fri.		
Sat.		
Sun.		

Weekly Total

Traveler's Training Log

Week _____ **Goal (Time/Distance)** _____ / _____

Day	Walking/Hiking Routes & Notes	Pulse Check*	Time hrs./min.	Distance (miles)
Mon.				
Tues.				
Wed.				
Thurs.				
Fri.				
Sat.				
Sun.				
* Heart rate after 20 minutes of walking/hiking		**Weekly Totals**		

Other Activities

Day		Time hrs./min.
Mon.		
Tues.		
Wed.		
Thurs.		
Fri.		
Sat.		
Sun.		
	Weekly Total	

Traveler's Training Log

Week _____   Goal (Time/Distance) _____ / _____

Day	Walking/Hiking Routes & Notes	Pulse Check*	Time hrs./min.	Distance (miles)
Mon.				
Tues.				
Wed.				
Thurs.				
Fri.				
Sat.				
Sun.				

* Heart rate after 20 minutes of walking/hiking

Weekly Totals

Other Activities

Time hrs./min.

Day	Activity	Time hrs./min.
Mon.		
Tues.		
Wed.		
Thurs.		
Fri.		
Sat.		
Sun.		

Weekly Total

Traveler's Training Log

Week _____   Goal (Time/Distance) _____ / _____

Day	Walking/Hiking Routes & Notes	Pulse Check*	Time hrs./min.	Distance (miles)
Mon.				
Tues.				
Wed.				
Thurs.				
Fri.				
Sat.				
Sun.				

* Heart rate after 20 minutes of walking/hiking

Weekly Totals

Other Activities

Time hrs./min.

Day	Activity	Time hrs./min.
Mon.		
Tues.		
Wed.		
Thurs.		
Fri.		
Sat.		
Sun.		

Weekly Total

Index